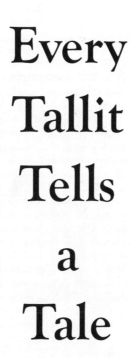

# Every
# Tallit
# Tells
# a
# Tale

### Debra W. Smith
### Editor

*Stella Hart, Inc.*

# Every Tallit Tells a Tale

**Stella Hart, Inc.**
**105 Shady Lane**
**Randolph, New Jersey 07869**

### Cataloging-in-Publication Data

Smith, Debra W.
Every Tallit Tells a Tale
ISBN 0-9768118-0-4
1. Tallitot—Jewish prayer shawls. 2. Jewish ritual practices.
3. Jewish autobiographical stories/memoirs.

Editorial production: Diana Drew
Cover art & interior art: Suzanne Warshavsky
Typesetting & layout: Wilma Martin

Printed in the United States of America.

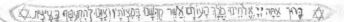

# Blessing for the Tzitzit

*It is customary to wrap oneself in the tallit before reciting the blessing that follows. After the blessing is recited, the tallit is placed across the shoulders. In some congregations, the blessing is said in unison.*

בָּרוּךְ אַתָּה יהוה אֱלֹהֵינוּ מֶלֶךְ הָעוֹלָם
אֲשֶׁר קִדְּשָׁנוּ בְּמִצְוֹתָיו
וְצִוָּנוּ לְהִתְעַטֵּף בַּצִיצִית:

Blessed are You, VEILED ONE, our God, the sovereign of all worlds, who has made us holy with your mitzvot, and commanded us to wrap ourselves amid the fringed tallit.

From *Kol Haneshamah: Shabbat Vehagim,* 3rd ed. Elkins Park, PA: The Reconstructionist Press, 2002. Reprinted with permission.

בָּרוּךְ אַתָּה יהוה אֱלֹהֵינוּ מֶלֶךְ הָעוֹלָם
אֲשֶׁר קִדְּשָׁנוּ בְּמִצְוֹתָיו
וְצִוָּנוּ לְהִתְעַטֵּף בַּצִיצִית:

Praised are You Adonai our God, who rules the universe, instilling in us the holiness of mitzvot by commanding us to wrap ourselves in *tzitzit.*

Reprinted from *Siddur Sim Shalom for Shabbat and Festivals,* © 1998, The Rabbinical Assembly.

To my mother, Estelle G. Weinberger, for all her support and for teaching me to always "Do what you love and love what you do."

# CONTENTS

\* \* \*

# Preface

Each essay or poem in *Every Tallit Tells a Tale* offers a distinctive snapshot, a glimpse of how a tallit figures in the writer's spiritual life. Most of these are poignant, heartfelt pieces—invitations into someone's deeply personal inner life.

The fringes of the tallit tie together generations within a family and generations within the larger family of all Jews. Tallitot inspire creativity in people who mesh their spiritual and creative urges as they weave or sew or knit prayer shawls for themselves or their loved ones. And for many writers—women especially—donning a tallit for the first time and uttering the age-old bracha, once exclusively reserved for men, takes on monumental significance. And, just as it does for men, the tallit brings these women closer to G-d; within its folds, they feel sheltered in divine warmth.

Collectively, the stories in *Every Tallit Tells a Tale* form an even larger picture. Like the individual brushstrokes in an impressionist painting, these individual stories blend into an image with its own meaning, its own contours. The image that emerges from reading these stories together reflects a traditional, yet evolving, Judaism. Our religion, our people, have been forever scarred by the Holocaust, yet we survive and even thrive in new lands. Stories about families handing down precious tallitot from generation to generation echo stories of tallitot that are the only remnants of families almost completely wiped out. Strands of world history, European history, and American history are interwoven from one tallit story to another. Well-traveled tallitot follow the path of wandering Jews from lands of persecution to lands of freedom.

Movements for a more inclusive Judaism form a backdrop to these personal stories, too, as women begin taking on the obligation of wearing the tallit, female rabbis and cantors grapple with the question of whether their personal faith requires them to don the tallit, and mothers create tallitot for their daughters and, later, themselves. These intensely personal decisions echo the drive for inclusion that we see evolving in the larger culture.

This collection includes stories from Israel as well. Born from the ashes of the Holocaust, Israel holds a cherished place in the Jewish imagination and in Jewish life. Yet these stories from Israel are of a piece with the others, as Jews both here and in Israel find their faith tested over and over again by challenges great and small, personal and political.

Every tallit *does* tell a tale, and each of those distinctive tales flows into the stream of Jewish history, enriching it in myriad ways. This prayer shawl figures in our most sacred moments—our B'nai and B'not Mitzvah, our weddings, our funerals. We commune with G-d in the comforting folds of the tallit. We finger the fringes as we pray for our families and our world. Woven into its very fabric are our hopes and dreams, our visions for the future, our memories of dear ones no longer with us. In draping the tallit on our shoulders, we forge our own connection to thousands of years of Jewish ritual and practice, now mingling with contemporary trends and sensibilities. Your story has a place here as well. What tale does your tallit tell?

—Diana Drew

# Acknowledgments

*E*very Tallit Tells a Tale was inspired by a spontaneous conversation with Dolly Grobstein and Jerry Krivitsky, two of my fellow congregants at Temple Shalom in Succasunna, New Jersey. My thanks to each of them for sharing the role their tallitot have played in shaping their Jewish lives.

Many people contributed helpful guidance at various stages in the writing of this book. In particular, I would like to express my sincerest appreciation to Fran Dyller, who proofread *Every Tallit Tells a Tale* and who also contributed by writing the text for the book's back cover. Eve Pasternak and Bracha Weisbarth, librarians at the Waldor Memorial Library at the United Jewish Communities of MetroWest in Whippany, New Jersey, were both an ongoing source of encouragement, support, and assistance as I was researching much of the background material I used in writing parts the book's Introduction.

My heartfelt appreciation to and admiration for everyone who contributed essays and poems to *Every Tallit Tells a Tale*. Thank you for sharing such intimate parts of your lives with me and for trusting me to share your stories with so many others.

*Every Tallit Tells a Tale* could not have come to fruition without the guidance, creativity, emotional support, and friendship of Diana Drew, the editorial director at my publishing house,

Stella Hart, Inc. My thanks as well to Stella Hart for her insights and encouragement in this project. Thank you both for believing in me and making my dream become a reality.

Several years ago I began a most incredible journey that has changed my life. My deepest gratitude and appreciation go to my rabbis and teachers who have traveled with me on the road back to being a committed, educated, and passionate Jew: Rabbis Judith Edelstein, Shoshanah Hantman, David Nesson, Joel Soffin, and Isaac Friedman, *z"l*, and to my teacher, colleague, and good friend, Dr. Mark Silk.

I also wish to acknowledge with gratitude my grand-parents, Hyman and Ida Galen and Regina Weinberger, for giving me my Jewish roots; and my family—my mother, Estelle Weinberger; my husband and companion on this journey, Dr. Neil Smith; and my daughters, Elana and Dana.

A very special thanks to my long-time and very dear friend, Elaine Luscombe, for her labor of love in making me my own unique "tallit of light," and to my daughter, Elana, who has been involved in each stage of its planning and design.

Above all, I thank G-d for guiding and sustaining me, and for showing me the way home.

—Debra W. Smith

# The Tallit:
# A Brief History & Overview

*Debra W. Smith*

*Speak to the Israelites and tell them they should make fringes on the corners of their garments for generations; they should place a twisted thread of blue on the corner fringes. It will be to you as fringes, and when you see it, you will remember all of the instructions of G-d and you will do them. You will not follow after your heart and after your eyes by which you are seduced. Thus you shall be reminded to do all My mitzvot and be holy to your G-d. (Numbers 15:38–40)*

Tallit (plural tallitot), or prayer shawl, is derived from the verb "to cover" in Hebrew and Aramaic. The word *tallit* originally meant "gown" or "cloak." A tallit is a loose, rectangular outer garment, usually made of either wool or linen. It resembles a blanket. One of the first biblical commandments given by G-d to Moses was to put fringes (tzitzit) on the corners of the garments. The most popular garment worn by the desert dwellers in biblical times to protect them from the extremes of climate was a rectangular blanket. In fact, the tallit is thought to resemble the abbayah (blanket) that was and still is worn by the desert-dwelling Bedouins.

It is said that the tallit is derived from the Roman pallium. During the Roman era (approximately 61 BCE–300 CE), a pallium with tzitzit attached to its corners was the trademark of wealthy and educated Jews and Christians. Wearing this garment distinguished them from pagans. Eventually, the pallium, reduced in size to a single strip of cloth resembling a scarf or stole, became a garment worn only by high-ranking officers on specified occasions. It is still worn by high dignitaries of the Christian church today. By a similar sequence of events, the pallium worn by Jews evolved into today's tallit. It became a ritual garment sometime after the Jewish dispersion from the Land of Israel.

Contemporary tallitot are made of wool or silk in a variety of colors and patterns. Among the techniques used to create and decorate tallitot today are quilting, weaving, knitting, appliqué, and tie-dyeing. Silk tallitot vary from fifty-four to ninety-six inches wide. The woolen tallit is larger, sometimes reaching to the ankle. The neckband or collar of the tallit is called the atarah (diadem). Oftentimes, the benediction recited when donning the tallit is woven right into the atarah. According to experts, the traditional design of the atarah is Spanish or Sephardic in origin. An alternative name for the atarah is the *spania*. From each of the four corners of the tallit hang the tzitzit (fringes). The only significance of the tallit itself is that the tzitziot (plural of *tzitzit*) hang from it. Independent of the tzitziot, the tallit has no religious importance. In order to be considered "kosher," a tallit may not be *sha'atnez*, a blend of wool and linen, which is prohibited by Jewish law.

Part of the mitzvah of the tzitzit is to incorporate a string of *techelet* (blue thread) among the fringes. *Techelet* is a type of blue dye that comes from a snail. Blue was used because it is the color of the sea and the sky. The knowledge of how to make the particular blue color was lost early in the Common Era, sometime around 600 CE. After this time, it became acceptable to use white threads alone.

You might notice people kissing the tzitzit several times during the prayer service. Just before the *Shema* is recited, the four tzitziot are gathered and held in one hand. It is customary to kiss the tzitzit three times during the recitation of Numbers 15:37–41, on those occasions when the word *tzitzit* is mentioned as part of the *Shema* prayer. When the kohanim (descendants of the priests) bestow the Priestly Blessing on the congregation, it is customary for them to cover their heads with their tallitot.

Tallitot have traditionally been worn by males, although there is no prohibition against women wearing them. More recently, women have begun to take on the obligation of wearing a tallit for prayer. For those of either gender who have accepted the obligation of wearing a tallit, the tallit is worn for prayer only at specified times: at every morning service, on the Sabbath, holy days, and weekdays (except on Tisha b'Av, when it is worn at the afternoon service). The tallit is not worn at either afternoon or evening services, except at the afternoon service on Tisha b'Av and on the eve of Yom Kippur (*Kol Nidre*). Many people wear an all-white tallit on the High Holy Days to symbolize purity.

Before donning the tallit, the following benediction is recited: "Praised are You, Adonai our G-d, who rules the universe, instilling in us the holiness of mitzvot by commanding us to wrap ourselves in *tzitzit*" (*Siddur Sim Shalom*). Some individuals raise the tallit over the head for a brief period after putting it on. Many people do this in order to take a few minutes to gather their thoughts and connect with G-d before the formal prayer experience.

Customs vary regarding who is expected to wear a tallit. In many Orthodox synagogues, a tallit is traditionally worn only by married men, although men may wear it when they are honored with an aliyah (that is, when they are called to the Torah). In more liberal Conservative and Reform congregations, the tallit may be worn by all men and women after the age of Bar or Bat Mitzvah.

Taking on the obligation of wearing a tallit is often a transformative experience. For the time that it embraces us, the tallit creates a sanctuary and a time of tranquility apart from the chaos of the everyday world. Wearing the tallit creates a boundary, or separation, in our lives. We are protected and we can commune with G-d; we can shut out all the rest, if even only for a little while.

Since taking on the obligation of wearing a tallit, I

have only once prayed without it and only twice prayed in a tallit that was not mine. My connection with G-d at those times was different from all the other prayer experiences I have had when praying in my own tallit. And it was only through those nonexperiences that I could begin to appreciate how important and how much a part of me my tallit has become. Reading and reviewing the stories for this book has shown me that so many others, of all ages, backgrounds, and lifestyles, feel the same way. We who have chosen to pray in tallitot perhaps comprise a self-selected and very unique family of Jews.

## SOURCES

Information for this essay comes from the following sources:

Donin, Rabbi Hayim Halevy. *To Pray as a Jew: A Guide to the Prayer Book and the Synagogue Service.* New York: Basic Books, A Division of Harper Collins Publishers, 1980.

*Encyclopedia Judaica Jerusalem*, vol. 15. Jerusalem: Keter Publishing House, Ltd./Macmillan, 1971.

Hammer, Reuven. *Entering Jewish Prayer: A Guide to Personal Devotion and the Worship Service.* New York: Schocken Books, 1994.

Ner-David, Haviva. "Tallit and Tallit Katan." In Rabbi Kerry M. Olitzky and Rabbi Daniel Judson, Eds. *The Rituals & Practices of a Jewish Life: A Handbook for Personal Spiritual Renewal.* Woodstock, VT: Jewish Lights Publishing, 2002.

Rubens, Alfred. *A History of Jewish Costume.* New York: Funk & Wagnalls, 1967.

# Introduction

## Debra W. Smith

June 12, 2004 was a glorious day. I sat in the stillness of the sanctuary, the sun streaming through the stained-glass windows, and watched eight of my students (ranging in age from mid-thirties to early seventies) prepare to experience a significant Jewish rite of passage. That day each of them would become a bat mitzvah. Six of the women donned tallitot and recited the blessing of the tzitzit. I was overcome with emotion and awe.

Only five years before, on the exact Hebrew date, I stood in a different sanctuary, on a different bimah, and donned my new tallit (given to me by my proud mother), as I became a bat mitzvah. Observing my students with pride, I knew my life had come full circle: I had grown from a marginal, complacent Jew to an observant one, from a student to a teacher, from a person whose spiritual life was often meaningless and bland to one filled with passion, direction, and a joy for waking up to bless each new day.

Looking at the women before me that day, I thought about how hard we had worked together over the past eighteen months to reach this moment in their lives. Like me, many of them had begun their studies with a desire to make the journey but with no knowledge of Hebrew. That glorious day, however, each of the women would lead parts of the Shabbat morning service and chant from the Torah. Some of the women had chosen to wear a tallit from that day on. Some knew that this *hiuv* (obligation) was one they would not undertake, while others wrestled with the question of whether to wear or not to wear a tallit up to the last moment.

I marched with the Torah procession that day as the women wound their way through the sanctuary, greeting family, friends, and community members. I stood on one side of the Torah scroll as the women chanted their Torah verses, and I hugged each of them as they finished. I reflected on how their journey was forever interwoven with my own, much like the strands of thread woven together on the tzitzit that some of us had chosen to wear.

My journey from the fringes of Judaism to its center has proceeded slowly. Only recently have I entered into a committed relationship with G-d. I'm not certain what prompted this change in my religious "status." Perhaps it was my need, in the midst of a full life, to connect with something beyond my immediate universe, to fill a nameless void in my soul. Ever so gradually, something unaccountable happened to me. I started to find and reclaim pieces of my life that I had never realized were missing: G-d and my Jewish voice.

As this evolution in my Jewish identity progressed, I felt compelled to learn all I could about every aspect of Judaism. This included learning the aleph-bet and how to read Hebrew; becoming familiar with the prayers and the order of the prayer service; studying how to chant from the Torah and also how to chant a Haftarah; exploring the Jewish life-cycle rituals; and delving into Jewish history and theology. At the same time, I decided to prepare to become a bat mitzvah (at the age of forty-six) and take on the obligation of wearing a tallit.

The first time I put on my tallit and recited the blessing of the tzitzit was early on in my Bat Mitzvah ceremony. It was a moment when time stopped, when I connected with my ancestors and claimed my place as one of many small links in the chain of Jewish history. I stood on the bimah that day fully cognizant that my life was about to change forever, that the choices I would make from that point on and the person I would grow to become would have very little in common with the person I had assumed I was throughout my life. This new person would be part of an eternal couple: my new life partner (in addition to my husband of more than twenty-five years) was G-d. I am truly fortunate that my husband understood and was more than willing to share our life together with another Presence who would be ever-present.

Each time I don my tallit is as meaningful as the first time. I continue to feel centered, focused, and embraced by G-d. My tallit also draws me into my community, to share the words of their prayers and to share my own with them. Enfolded in my tallit, I pray with kavannah (intention) and focus. Although mine is not a specially commissioned tallit, it has traveled every step of the way with me on my Jewish journey. It has comforted and embraced me during prayers of joy and sorrow, fear, anger, and even whispers of doubt. I have worn it when I became a bat mitzvah, as a student of prayer, and now as a teacher and *ba'alat t'fila* (prayer leader) with a community of my own.

My tallit and I have matured together and the aging process shows on both of us. I have more wrinkles, aches, and gray hairs; my tallit is frayed, worn, and stained with lipstick from the kisses it receives as we regularly prepare to meet G-d together in prayers of praise, petition, and thanksgiving. My tallit and I have come to share a history. Whenever I put my tallit on, it molds to my body; likewise, I mold to its form as it continues to shape my Jewish identity.

As my tallit and I sat together waiting for services to begin one recent Shabbat morning, I turned to the woman seated on my left, whom I didn't know. She was wearing an eye-catching tallit with colored stripes and so, as a way of greeting her, I asked where she had found her tallit. She shared a fascinating story with me and concluded by saying, "If you think my story is interesting, talk to him," pointing to the man sitting on my right. When I asked him to tell me about his tallit, he dismissed my question quickly by saying there really was no story behind his tallit: He had simply purchased it on a family trip to Israel. "Oh," I replied, feeling sheepish for having asked. Literally a heartbeat later, he tapped me on the arm and said, "What I told you wasn't true. This tallit has changed my life."

He proceeded to tell me how.

I thought about his words throughout the service. And as I rode home, the idea for *Every Tallit Tells a Tale* took shape. Whether or not every tallit story is memorable and worthy of publishing, I believe that every tallit has a story to tell. It is our responsibility as their "keepers" and partners to be the vehicle through which the tales of our silent (but nonetheless powerful) partners are shared with others.

Each of us has unique experiences of G-d's grace. All the contributors to this volume have had a tallit figure in their experiences of the Divine. Whether it was as the creator of a custom-made tallit for a beloved niece on the occasion of her Bat Mitzvah, the heir of a father's precious tallit, or the way a tallit helped a woman channel her late father in writing a letter that saved her life, the writers whose stories fill this book share a sense that the tallit adds meaning, divine blessing, and spiritual depth to their lives.

The tallit also evokes sensory memories for many of the writers—a wool tallit scratching the skin, the cool silk of a tallit skimming their shul clothes, a multicolored Israeli tallit that lifts their mood and lifts their spirits each time it's pulled from its precious matching bag, caressed and kissed, and gently draped around the shoulders.

The stories are touching, poignant, and inspiring, all pointing up ways a simple prayer shawl, imbued with a divine imprimatur, brings us closer to G-d and ignites the often-dormant divine spark within us.

## A Word About Language

I use the word *tallit*, rather than *tallis*, in the title and throughout this book, reflecting the Sephardic pronunciation of the Hebrew letter *taf*. This accords with modern Hebrew pronunciation. In Ashkenazi circles (among people from Eastern Europe), *taf* is pronounced *saf*, so *tallit* becomes *tallis* and the plural *tallitot* becomes *tallasim*. Several of the contributors to the book use the Ashkenazi spelling because the person whose tallit is being described always referred to the prayer shawl that way.

# My Journey
# from the Fringe to the Fringes

## Debra W. Smith

*Blessed are You, Adonai, our G-d. Be with me as I prepare to enfold myself in Your loving embrace. Watch over me as I pray. Inspire me to help heal the world, bring peace to others, and repair my own brokenness.*

Community membership is an integral part of Jewish life, one that helps us define ourselves as individuals and in our relationship with G-d. Belonging to a synagogue and to a Jewish community was something I always had taken for granted, until my husband and I, and our two-year-old daughter, Elana, moved to Long Valley, New Jersey, in 1982.

As we settled in, we quickly became aware that the demographics of Long Valley and its environs included fewer than a dozen Jewish families. We sought out, visited, and joined a "local" synagogue, attended services there sporadically, and remained marginally involved with the synagogue community during our five-year membership. While I continued to celebrate Hanukkah and Rosh Hashanah, to observe Yom Kippur, and to attend an annual Passover seder, I became increasingly removed from Judaism and didn't feel a part of the larger (or even the more local) Jewish community. I began to feel estranged and disconnected from Judaism, and ever more alone. I was living on the fringe of Jewish life, and that caused me great pain.

The years passed. I completed graduate school, launched a career as a family therapist, and had a second child. What persisted, however, was that vague feeling of unsettled-ness and lack of connection to Judaism. My pain wasn't acute, but it was always there, a dull ache, a heaviness in my heart. We joined another synagogue. Perhaps, we thought, we'd feel more part of the community in a smaller place.

Our elder daughter became a bat mitzvah in that smaller synagogue and we remained affiliated for a brief time. Then we moved on. This also was not a community to which we felt connected. The emotional ache, now an integral part of me, persisted, as did our family's hovering on the fringe of Judaism.

Now with a second daughter, Dana, to educate, we moved to yet a third congregation. It was there that I met a newly ordained, middle-aged, female rabbi who changed my life. She offered me—and I tentatively accepted—the slightly tarnished jewel of Judaism that I eventually made my own. Thus my Jewish journey began in earnest. A most significant part of that journey included preparing for and becoming a bat mitzvah myself.

Accepting the *hiuv* (obligation) of wearing a tallit was a natural step for me. I enter into G-d's intimate embrace and renew my commitment to G-d as I don my tallit and kiss its fringes during the *Shema*. I have never prayed without my beloved tallit since the day I became a bat mitzvah. The feeling of awe and reverence for G-d remains ever-present as I enfold myself in my tallit and prepare to pray.

Two years post–Bat Mitzvah, I was deeply entrenched in synagogue and ritual life and had a new-found career in Jewish education that I loved. Despite my Bat Mitzvah, however, I didn't feel any less on the fringe of our current synagogue community. It, too, was not the right spiritual center for our family. At this point in my spiritual path, I was an observant, passionately

committed Jew, and I needed to find the right community, one in which I could feel supported and spiritually at
home. Several of my colleagues in the field of Jewish
education took it upon themselves to help our family in
the quest to find the right community—a religious
"home," a place where we could pray, study Torah,
engage in acts of *gemilut hasadim* (loving-kindness), and
even have a good time. We saw ourselves running out of
options; we were truly giving new meaning to the
phrase "wandering Jews"! We were also spiritually
exhausted from moving from one synagogue to another,
and longed to find a permanent home.

However, we were not feeling confident in our ability to make a choice. Making a Solomonic decision, we
joined two congregations—one Conservative and one
Reform—each with wonderful attributes and each with
outstanding rabbis. We receive spiritual nourishment
and inspiration in both places, and we consider ourselves doubly blessed.

IN THE SPIRIT of *gemilut hasadim*, Rabbi Joel Soffin of our
Reform community, Temple Shalom, in Succasunna,
New Jersey, created a social action project called Shalom
Ethiopia. He returned from his mission to Ethiopia with
beautiful, vibrantly colored tallit bags made by
Ethiopian Jews. I was delighted to find and purchase
one with the biblical heroine Deborah (my namesake) on
it. Midrash tells us that Deborah is known as a woman
of flames and light—an *eshet lapidote*. Deborah's fiery
energy has become an inspiration to me on my Jewish
journey. Hearing and teaching Deborah's story has given
me the courage to approach many personal fires without
worrying about getting burned, has empowered me to
not draw back from the intensity of the heat, and has
enabled me to use the light to see the world with greater
clarity.

Only after bringing this beautiful and inspirational
tallit bag home did I realize that while I could put my
tallit inside it, the two items—my tallit and this new

bag—didn't go together. The whole union—old tallit and new tallit bag—just felt all wrong. There was no symmetry, either emotionally or from an artistic point of view. No way could my American-made tallit live in this Ethiopian tallit bag! Feeling deflated, I put the bag in my closet, thinking I would give it as a gift one day.

In time, my family and I have become more involved with Temple Shalom's social action efforts in Ethiopia. Recently, we made the decision to "adopt" (financially support) an Ethiopian child. In fact, the photograph of our six-year-old "son," Sammy, along with his health status report, hangs on our refrigerator along with photos of our daughters, nieces, nephews, and cousins.

Shalom Ethiopia, and the commitment of the Temple Shalom synagogue community to this project, has served as an inspiration to me in my own work in the Jewish community. It has added another dimension to my own spiritual journey and enriched my relationship with G-d. I have come to see the world and G-d's presence in that world in a different light. I have been energized to start a number of social action projects of my own. The senior community where I work as adult Jewish educator and lay leader is now involved in many worthwhile *tikkun olam* projects locally, in Israel, and in Ethiopia.

Most recently, my husband asked me to take a look at the Ethiopian tallitot at Temple Shalom because he wished to purchase a new tallit for himself. As I looked through the samples, I noticed a tallit lying by itself in a corner at the far side of the room. Was this ritual garment, much like me, residing on the fringe, not quite a part of the other sample tallitot the synagogue had? It was not one of the samples the rabbi chose to show me, so I asked, "What about that one? Is that one an option?"

The rabbi picked it up and, as he stretched it lengthwise for me to see, he said, "It looks kind of small for your husband."

"But," I countered, "it is perfect for me! I'll take it!" I noticed right away how perfectly this tallit matched the tallit bag that now resided in my closet. I tried it on quickly, folded it up ever so carefully, took it home and put it to rest in the tallit bag with Deborah's picture on it—where it truly belongs! Now the tallit, like its new owner, has found a permanent home. Neither of us has to reside on the fringe of Judaism any longer!

FEBRUARY 19, 2005: What better time for my new tallit to make its debut than Shabbat Tetzaveh? This Torah portion focuses on the significance of each item of clothing to be worn by the *kohain gadole* (high priest) and the other kohanim. And what better place for me to don my new tallit for the first time than at the Lester Senior Community in Whippany, New Jersey? I have had the privilege of serving as the Adult Jewish Educator and Lay Leader of this wonderful community for the past two years. During that time, we have grown to be a close-knit group through praying, studying, and engaging in works of *tikkun olam* together.

It was only natural for me to announce before beginning services that I wanted to share a special occasion in my life with them. I removed my new tallit from its bag and began to talk about its journey and mine, and how our paths had recently crossed. I also said that while I have studied long and hard in many venues over the past years since returning to Judaism, nothing has nourished my growth more than their community. Through leading them in prayer, I have grown immeasurably as a spiritual leader; through studying with them and teaching them, I have come to define myself as a credible Jewish educator; through our social action projects, I have learned to see the world around me from a different perspective. Their support has allowed me to respond to G-d's calling. We have become each other's spiritual community.

The sanctuary was so still that time seemed to stop during those few minutes that I spoke. I then recited the blessing, kissed each side of the atarah, turned away from the congregation, and draped the tallit over my head for a long moment. I turned toward my community, recited the *Shehecheyanu*, took a deep breath and invited them to join me in prayer. Aloud, I said, "We now rise to begin our service with the Blessings of Renewal."

Silently, I said, "Thank you, G-d, for not letting me turn back when the going has been so hard that I have wanted to run from You."

And so my journey continues. I wonder what awaits me next . . .

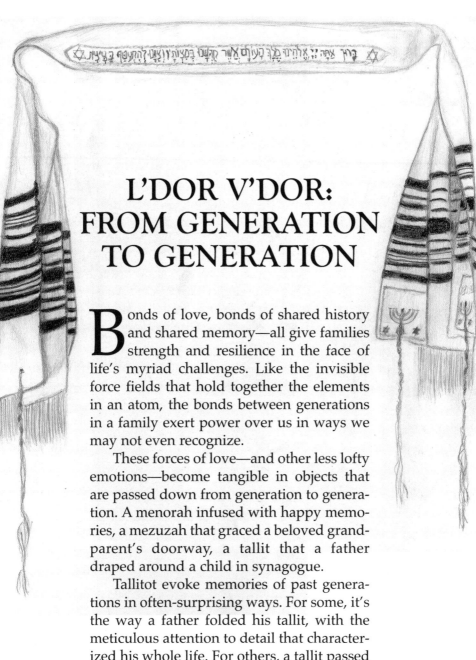

# L'DOR V'DOR: FROM GENERATION TO GENERATION

**B**onds of love, bonds of shared history and shared memory—all give families strength and resilience in the face of life's myriad challenges. Like the invisible force fields that hold together the elements in an atom, the bonds between generations in a family exert power over us in ways we may not even recognize.

These forces of love—and other less lofty emotions—become tangible in objects that are passed down from generation to generation. A menorah infused with happy memories, a mezuzah that graced a beloved grandparent's doorway, a tallit that a father draped around a child in synagogue.

Tallitot evoke memories of past generations in often-surprising ways. For some, it's the way a father folded his tallit, with the meticulous attention to detail that characterized his whole life. For others, a tallit passed down from father to son—now frayed, and worn only on holidays—blends past and present, as the middle-aged heir to the tallit sees his father once again as he glimpses his own image, swathed in the tallit. A tallit, worn by the father, now falls easily on the son's shoulders, in a tradition that stretches back thousands of years.

New traditions, for generations yet to come, are being created today as women embrace the tallit. Many women now find spiritual solace and connection to God in donning a tallit themselves or bestowing one on a beloved daughter at her Bat Mitzvah, ushering her into a fledgling sisterhood of female tallit-wearers.

This prayer shawl, which hangs lightly on the shoulders, bears the weight of highly charged memories with ease and grace. The contributors to this section feel the spirit of a loved one in the weave and tzitzit of a tallit.

The biblical injunction to wear tzitzit suffuses this sacred shawl with holiness and God's love. And just as divine love threads through individual lives, the love and memories that tie one generation to another can be traced through the fabric of a tallit.

—Diana Drew

# A Tallit Imbued with Hope

*Howard Siegel*

Barely seventeen years old, Ely was experiencing a wide range of conflicting emotions, from ice-cold fear and morbid trepidation, to frissons of excitement and teenage wonderment. Having never been on a ship before, Ely watched and listened in a state of pure awe as the massive ship prepared to get under way. It was hard enough for him to be going to America, but he was going there absolutely alone. He did not know a single passenger on the ship. Suddenly, a feeling of foreboding swept over the young man, as it struck him that he might never see his parents, his other relatives, or his friends ever again.

However, he knew what he had to do, for the situation in Kiev in 1912 had become exceedingly dangerous. Religious intolerance had evolved into religious persecution. Civil and political chaos sanctioned robbery and murder, and proceeded unchecked and unpunished. In addition, Ely and his parents wanted no part of the corrupt Russian military conscription system. The young and able needed to leave Kiev while there was still a chance to make a life for themselves elsewhere.

As the ship pulled away from the pier and headed for the open sea, Ely clutched his few possessions. The most treasured reminder of his Jewish faith was his tallit, which now offered him a measure of comfort and reassurance. Ely caressed the prized prayer shawl, which had been folded with care and placed in his small cloth bag. He wrapped his fingers around the fringes, and recited the prayer for a safe journey. As was the custom in Kiev, Ely had not become Bar Mitzvah in the sense that we practice this rite of passage today; rather, he had simply been presented with a tallit by his family, and invited to read from the Torah on Shabbat. This had been a wonderful experience for Ely, and his tallit was his only tangible connection to that special Shabbat morning. Ely took great care to keep his tallit properly folded and scrupulously clean. After all, he wore it while praying to G-d, so only the very best was acceptable. He would periodically check the material, the knots, and the fringes for any separation, fraying, or tears. When the memory of that Shabbat morning—the first time he had been called to the Torah—started to fade, his tallit would suddenly bring everything back into sharp focus.

Ely had been a serious student of Torah at a yeshiva in Kiev, and his parents thought he possessed a photographic memory. Growing up in Kiev turned boys into men at a very young age. Physical labor and daily chores were coupled with Torah study. Most boys started working at the age of seven. Ely had a deep sense of personal responsibility, and worked hard at all his assigned tasks. As the ship headed west, toward Ely's new life, the smooth, silky texture of his tallit felt good, almost like a tonic, in his calloused hands. He clutched the tallit even tighter as the ship began to roll in the foaming sea. While some view a tallit simply as a piece of material with fringes, Ely thought of it as a symbol of what he had become: as strong as the stringed fringes, respectful and reverent as the embossed bracha, and deeply cognizant of the history and traditions of his Jewish faith.

Ely knew that whatever he chose to do, he would have many more opportunities in America, and he was grateful that his parents had given him this precious chance. Still clutching the tallit, Ely found that the images of his parents, relatives, and friends had faded. It seemed like such a long time ago that his parents had been anxiously clutching his shoulders, whispering prayers and advice. He was now alone on the high seas; however, he had his tallit, and that would have to see him through many seasick days before he reached New York harbor. Something told him to hold onto that tallit—not to lose it, or leave it behind—that future generations would want and need it.

Through years of working in restaurants, opening his own restaurant, raising a family, and always giving back to the community, Ely never faltered in practicing the watchwords of his beloved faith. He kept his tallit from Kiev in a safe place. While most Jewish men "graduate" to at least one other tallit during their lifetime, Ely preferred to use the tallit he had brought from Kiev. The tallit had become his lifelong companion and confidante, because they had both been through so much together.

The years passed, and one generation replaced another. It is a long time and distance from Ely's youth in Kiev to contemporary Atlanta, but sometimes there is a bridge to span this great divide. The Walden family, in discussing B'nai Mitzvah plans for their sons, Michael and Danny, who happen to be my favorite nephews, were looking for ways to observe this meaningful and memorable occasion. What better family possession to have at the B'nai Mitzvah than Great-Grandfather Ely's tallit from Kiev! What better way to show their profound respect and admiration for an ancestor who, as a young boy, gave so much of himself so that all of us could carry on our Code of Jewish Law with dignity, respect, and honor.

Ely's tallit rested on the bookstand while Danny and Michael read their individual portions. The significance and meaning of Ely's well-traveled tallit was explained to those in attendance. Some of the attendees were astonished at the history of the tallit: Its survival over all those miles and all those years was itself a miracle. In a throwaway society, how did the tallit survive?

The tallit survived because the family wanted it to survive, and took the necessary steps to ensure that it would remain safe and sound. I did not know Ely personally, but I believe that he nurtured the tallit as if it possessed a soul, as if it would help us to understand that our religious beliefs transcend time, distance, and generations. Even though we live in a world light years away from 1912 Kiev, the tallit serves as a symbol of our abiding faith and remembrance.

Ely was correct: Future generations did want and need the tallit. It is now our responsibility to care for it for future generations.

**Howard Siegel** lives in the Cleveland area, and belongs to Temple Emanu El. He has had articles published in a number of periodicals, including the *Cleveland Jewish News* and *Generations*, the Magazine of the Jewish Museum of Maryland.

# Through My Mother's Tears

*Linda Hoffman Kay*

Who could have imagined? My son, Eric Jordan Kay, became a bar mitzvah on May 19, 2002, at Temple Beth Am in Parsippany, New Jersey. We said the blessing and wrapped him in his beautiful tallit with blue and white embroidery that we had purchased at our synagogue gift shop along with a matching bag. We held our breath and stepped back.

Eric stood on the bimah, age thirteen years and three months, looked out at the congregation, and, without blinking an eye, conducted the service along with the rabbi. He sang the *Shema* and *V'ahavta* with his beautiful soprano voice. He chanted the Torah blessings and his Torah portion with ease. He recited the Haftarah blessings, read his portion in English, and gave a sermon about his household responsibilities and how he was going to learn to do the laundry. That elicited a few laughs from the congregation. He paused appropriately during the laughter. He made no mistakes, didn't get flustered, and clearly took pride in his monumental achievement. It was, as my mother said to me, the happiest day of her life.

I SOBBED ON the way home from the child development center. We had just endured several months of testing of our beautiful two-year-old son who didn't talk, didn't interact, and didn't know how to engage in imaginary play. He was my third child, already followed by a sister, born sixteen months after him. He had been such an easy baby, one who loved to sit quietly and play with colored blocks—categorizing them by color or shape. He was a relief after his two older, active brothers. I hadn't noticed that he didn't respond when his name was called or when he was asked "Where's … ?" What did bother me was that he didn't speak.

That began our journey to have his hearing tested (normal), and then a speech evaluation at a local hospital. The red flags went up, and every professional at the center began to analyze him. Now we had a label—pervasive developmental disorder, not otherwise specified, or PDDNOS, as it was affectionately called in the DSM IV-R. I mulled over the words in the report that stated that my baby needed to be educated in programs for children with autism. My husband gently reminded me that he was still the same child we loved the day before we knew he had a label.

My mother told me two things that helped me get on the right course: (1) I needed to meet other mothers in the same situation as soon as possible, and (2) I would be able to do everything possible to help overcome this heartbreaking diagnosis. I was determined that day to save him. And my mother was right: As soon as we began early intervention, I met those other mothers like me. My son slowly began to respond to language as he worked with his first teachers.

THUS BEGAN OUR journey through special education and years of private speech therapy. He knew a few words by three years old, put words together at four, and slowly but surely, began to speak, albeit unintelligibly. Miraculously, he learned to read and articulate at age seven and the world began to open up to him. You see, said my mother, all of your hard work is paying off.

Jewish education soon followed. It began in a specialized Sunday program for children with disabilities and continued at our synagogue religious school where he was accompanied and tutored by a compassionate teenage girl who was a member of our congregation. Since we attended services regularly, he learned all the prayers by heart. When it came time for his Bar Mitzvah preparations, I was able to tutor him at home and color-coded similar words in his Torah portion to help him remember his lines.

And so, it was a great joy to choose the tallit that would adorn his shoulders on that special day. And it was even a greater joy to know that Eric could wear that tallit, become a bar mitzvah, and participate as fully as any of his "typical" peers.

I sang "When You Believe" from *The Prince of Egypt* as my parental blessing to Eric on his Bar Mitzvah day. I looked at my mother, who held back the cough that had plagued her for several months. Her eyes, and those of others were filled with tears. Tears of joy.

*In loving memory of my mother, Bernice Lillian Hoffman, Beilah bat Reuven v'Michal, z"l.*

**Linda Hoffman Kay** lives in Parsippany, New Jersey, where she is a member of Temple Beth Am, Parsippany. She is an associate at the Jewish Education Association of MetroWest Center for Special Education, where she oversees programs for children, parents, and educators. She and her husband David are the parents of Daniel, Jonathan, Eric, and Lauren.

# My Father's Tallit

*Rabbi Evan Radler*

My father had an advanced Yeshiva education and was ordained a rabbi, although he never worked as one. He owned many *siddurim* (prayer books) and many *sforim* (scholarly texts), a pair of tefillin (phylacteries); and two huge woolen tallitot, one for everyday use and one for Shabbat and yom tov (holidays), both in the traditional style of black stripes on white.

I have an early memory, perhaps pre-language, of sitting in my father's lap with his arms and huge woolen tallit draped around me. I still remember clearly a feeling that was surely wordless at the time and even forty or so years later defies description. It was a feeling of absolute security and unconditional love. Later, when I was old enough to occupy my own seat but still too young to appreciate the divine blessing that is air conditioning, my father would drape one end of his great woolen tallit over me to keep me warm. The tallit felt warm and cozy and always had the scent of my father's cologne.

When I was growing up, everything in synagogue was natural. My father never told me to be quiet or pay attention. He would hold the book for me and point to the words. If I followed the prayers, that was good. If mind and eye wandered, that was alright too. I can still remember my father's finger on the page. Often, I just watched that finger, adorned with a writing callous, rather than following the words. To this day, when reading a Hebrew text, I often still see that calloused finger on the page.

On weekday mornings I was awakened by the gentle brush of tzitzit (the biblically mandated fringes on the four corners of the tallit) upon my cheek. My first sight each morning was of my father in full regalia of tallit and tefillin. He greeted each day by first greeting his Maker, alone in the lingering gray of pre-dawn. From boyhood I learned to think of tefillin and the great tallit as the trappings of manhood.

I witnessed the extraordinary care lavished on those holy vestments. It seemed to me at the time that it was an extension of the ritual. Dad took quite good care of everything he owned. Clothing was neatly folded and put away. Books were never left out on the table; they were shelved in their specific places immediately after use. It wasn't only compulsion. It was a respect for tangible things that was an extension of self-respect. He often marveled—in later years silently—at my almost total lack of that same respect.

There was nothing to compare with the absolutely meticulous procedure of folding the giant tallit. The holy sheet would be folded, refolded, and folded yet again until it was as neat and tight as a flag fit for presentation by an Eagle Scout. Then and only then would my father replace it in the soft velvet case beside the tefillin.

At a certain point I became a participant in this part of the ritual. My father would hold two corners of the garment and I would hold two. The tallit would be pulled taut and we would shake out the wrinkles and creases of its most recent use. Then we would walk toward each other, matching corner to corner, and repeat the process with the now-halved sheet. We continued this little dance for three turns until the tallit was more easily manageable by one person. Of course, each of these folds would certainly be repeated if it were not perfect.

My father had his first heart attack at the age of forty-five. I was fourteen at the time. Bypass surgery and other techniques were not as advanced in the 1970s as they are now, and the prognosis was not good. Dad asked for his weekday tallit to be kept on the table beside his bed, even though he was not in a position to don it.

One evening, after returning by bicycle from a visit to my father in the hospital, I took out the Shabbat tallit. I didn't unfold it; I just held the neatly bundled vestment up to my face and inhaled my father's cologne. I prayed to God silently that this tallit would not become mine any time soon. I wept into the bundle and swore to my Maker many solemn vows, all probably unfulfilled and now long forgotten.

I have found in my personal experience that God does answer "Yes" to many prayers—not to all and perhaps not to most, but to many. The tallit would not be mine for another twenty years.

On the night before I inherited that tallit, I visited my father in the hospital. He had been in and out of the hospital now and again in the intervening years. There didn't seem to be any reason to believe that at age sixty-five, this time would be any different. The velvet tallit bag was beside him on a chair. When I asked him how he felt, as usual he had no complaints, only inquiries as to how I was doing. It seemed ridiculous that the man with the heart condition, lying in a hospital bed would presume to be just fine and ask about the condition of the healthy man standing before him. I have since realized that some people who stand straight and tall are not doing so well, while many on their deathbeds are really doing just fine. We hugged, said good-night, and I told him I would return tomorrow. He told me only to come if I had time and I wasn't too tired.

My father passed through the veil to the next world early the following morning. I spent the day driving my mother on those essential errands after a death, including delivering one tallit to the funeral home. We decided that Dad's everyday tallit would accompany his earthly remains and that his only child would inherit the Shabbat and yom tov tallit, along with his many books and other Judaic items, most of which he had given to me as gifts over the years while he was still alive.

Less than a month later came the High Holy Days. At services in the synagogue I took out the tallit. I held the fringes on the four corners together and draped the still partially folded mantel over one shoulder, as I had been taught by my father and who in turn had been taught to do it this way by his father. I intoned the blessing with more feeling than ever before. When I wrapped myself in the tallit, a lifetime of memories came flooding through me. There inside the tallit I remembered the warmth, the safety, and the unconditional love. I remembered my first feelings about God, Judaism, the synagogue, and, of course, my father. I had a loving, caring, devoted father, so I grew up believing in a loving, caring, devoted God.

I next intoned the blessing of *Shehecheyanu*, recited when wearing something new. This tallit was older than I was, but it was new to me. After intoning the blessings, I whispered, "Thanks, Dad."

I have never quite mastered the art of folding that tallit the way my father did. I noticed soon after I took to wearing it on all Sabbaths and holidays that it seemed to be wearing out more in a few months in my charge than it had during several decades in my father's care. I put it away and wear it but once a year at some time over the High Holy Days. It is now eight years that the tallit is mine and I'm sure that I still detect the faintest trace of my father's cologne.

**Rabbi Evan Radler**, who passed away suddenly in 2005, served Conservative congregations in New York and Georgia since his ordination at Yeshiva University at age twenty-five. At the time he wrote this essay, he was the spiritual leader at the Hillcrest Jewish Center in Queens.

# My Grandfather's Tallit

## Robert Grayson

I was still in diapers when my grandfather, Sol Engelhard, first took me to synagogue. I was his eldest grandchild, and he brought me to shul on Shabbat week after week and on other holidays as well. While I can't remember my first appearance at services, I do remember sitting with my grandfather in the sukkah, and marching in the synagogue with a flag and an apple on Simchat Torah, and the congregants hissing during the recitation of the Megillat Esther on Purim whenever the name *Haman* was mentioned.

In Brooklyn, where I grew up, Jewish people felt children should be exposed to their religion at a young age. During the 1950s, the extended family was very important, and grandparents played an important role in their grandchildren's lives. Grandfathers felt it was their responsibility to take their grandsons to synagogue. And since my parents and I lived only a few blocks away from my grandparents in the Flatbush section of Brooklyn, I was able to accompany my grandfather to services frequently.

At seven years old, I was a well-behaved child. In those days, children who didn't behave at services were politely ushered outside. But I sat quietly, and I usually stayed in the sanctuary for the entire service—something that made my grandfather very proud.

One reason I sat quietly was because I was under the impression that the kiddush at the end of the service was only for the well-behaved. Therefore, there'd be no cake for anyone who carried on. And not only did I look forward to having a piece of cake myself, but I also eagerly anticipated taking a piece of cake home to my mom. I learned this from my grandfather. Each Shabbat, before we left the synagogue after services, he would wrap up a piece of cake in a napkin and take it home to my grandmother. So, naturally, I would wrap up a piece of cake to take home to my mom, which I gave her permission to share with my father if he wasn't at services.

One of the hardest parts of the Shabbat service to sit through quietly was the rabbi's sermon. In Brooklyn, rabbis always gave long sermons. Though no one would admit it, I did see grown men dozing off during the sermon. My grandfather told me that they were "concentrating." But I found the sermons boring. And I really needed something to do as the rabbi droned on.

So I decided to work on answering one of the great questions of all time: How many tzitzit hung from my grandfather's tallit?

Following the Torah reading every Sabbath, as the crowd started to hush so the rabbi could speak, I would begin the endless task of counting the tzitzit in hopes of one day coming up with a definitive answer. (I didn't realize, of course, that the answer had been known for centuries—613, the number of mitzvot Jewish men are required to perform. This information was something you learned when you became bar mitzvah.)

Counting the tzitzit was very tedious work. My grandfather had an old tallit that I always remember him wearing. It was the traditional white and blue tallit and was a bit weathered with age, which meant the tzitzit strands would sometimes stick together like spaghetti that had been cooked too long.

I would always make sure that he took the same tallit every Shabbat. There were tallitot at the synagogue if you forgot your own. But I wanted to count the tzitzit on his tallit, because if he used one from the synagogue the number of tzitzit wouldn't have been the same (so I thought).

Lots of things happen when you count tzitzit at seven years old. You lose count a lot and have to start over. But that's OK. There was plenty of time. You have to make sure that you properly separate the counted strands from the uncounted ones. If a person moves, you might have to start all over again. When the tallit strands stick together, you're often distracted by pulling them apart, and have to start the count all over again. And you want to work very gently. You don't want to disturb the tallit wearer, and you certainly don't want him to know you're not paying attention to every word the rabbi's saying. So, to some degree, this is a clandestine operation. There are times you want to sit on the tallit wearer's right side, and times you want to be on the left side, so you can count both sides.

You have to keenly develop your memory because it is the Sabbath, and you cannot write down the numbers that you count. Therefore, you have to rely on your memory for the count to proceed properly.

My early math teachers always told me that you had to "check your work" when it comes to numbers. So I knew that, before I came up with the definitive tzitzit number, I would have to recount to check my work before any official pronouncement could be made. I was utterly convinced that this task could be accomplished, even if no one else had done it before.

I proceeded with my work diligently Sabbath after Sabbath, thoroughly convinced that my task was being carried out with the utmost secrecy, no one aware of what I was doing or the ingenious way I had developed to sit quietly as the rabbi spoke about something I couldn't understand.

So you can imagine my shock and dismay, after putting all this time into tzitzit counting, when my grandfather told me one day that he had gotten a new tallit. After showing me the tallit, with the bright bracha on the atarah, the brilliant blue color, and the sharp new tzitzit, my grandfather said to me with his reassuring smile, "Now you're going to have to start counting the tzitzit all over again."

**Robert Grayson**, an award-winning sportswriter and public relations executive, looks back on Brooklyn in the 1950s as halcyon days in a charmed place: Children were everywhere (this was the baby boom generation), the Dodgers played at Ebbets Field, all was right with the world. As a child, Mr. Grayson thought that everyone was Jewish (even Mickey Mantle!) because everyone in his neighborhood was Jewish. He and his wife, Diana Drew, live in Randolph, New Jersey.

# My Tallit Mitzvah

*Marcia Bronstein*

The tallit I wear is unlike the old-fashioned blue and white satin tallit my grandfather Abraham wore. Mine is beige, a simple weave that looks like lace, and rests neatly on my shoulders. I feel a connection to the unbroken chain of the Jewish people each time I think about it.

When I was a child, I used to walk my grandfather to and from shul and I was always full of questions for him. Almost every answer to my questions was, "It is not your obligation, Marshinka." Patiently and lovingly, he would explain that Jewish men and women have different obligations, and women were not bound to follow the time-honored commandments.

My grandfather, a cantor who gave up his cantorial pursuits when he immigrated to New York from Argentina via Russia, made his living as a printer and fed his soul as a cantor during the High Holy Days. He traveled to various communities around New York each fall to do what he loved—to sing and read Torah. I remember how he practiced each parashah. He did it when he raked the leaves, when he walked home from the subway, and when he was sitting under a tree enjoying a breeze on a summer day.

My grandfather would have been proud when I celebrated my Bat Mitzvah in 2004. He had died in 1980 without ever teaching me the trope or how to sing the parashot. He never taught me how to lift or dress the Torah. Those were things that were not the *minhag ha macom* (custom) in the shul where I grew up. When I was called to the Torah for the first time at my Bat Mitzvah on May 29, 2004, I had hoped to do it wearing my grandfather's tallit.

Unfortunately, that was not to be. No one seemed to know what had become of the blue and white satin tallit stored in the blue velvet tallit bag that my grandfather carried. With all the mourning and sadness surrounding his death, relatives, meaning to be helpful, came to assist my grandmother in cleaning out things that were not going to be needed once she moved. In their zeal to scale back the household, many of my grandfather's prized possessions were misplaced or given away.

I still feel pangs of sadness when I think about the full collection of leather-bound Sholom Aleichem books in Yiddish that were supposed to be mine. Somehow they ended up in my uncle's garage, where they became water-damaged beyond salvaging. I learned about this four years later when I was ready to incorporate them into my household after I was married. The books, often verbally earmarked as a gift to me from my grandparents, were a bridge from their lives in Russia to their new existence in America. I was to inherit them because I was a graduate of the Sholom Aleichem Folk Shule and spoke and read Yiddish. They hoped that the Yiddish wisdom and stories would somehow be translated to future generations of our family, and they were entrusting me with this task. It was an obligation that I was eager to assume.

I think that both my grandparents would have been delighted that I decided at age forty-five to become a bat mitzvah. I had never been completely comfortable with accepting an aliyah and being called to the Torah. I felt that I should confront my feelings by lifting the Torah during what I think is the most meaningful part of the Torah service—*Zot ha Torah* . . . (This is the Torah)—which reminds us that this was the Torah that God gave to Moses. I was nervous. I had more angst about lifting the Torah than I did about reading from the Torah. I had practiced lifting the Torah, and had almost given up the idea because I had hurt my back the first time I had practiced it. (Bending at the knees and using the table to push off are key.)

When it was my turn to lift the Torah, I walked up to the bimah and confidently lifted the Torah, held it high for all to see, and then sat down so it could be properly dressed. The entire time, I was filled with joy, remembering all the times my grandfather had helped me to kiss the Torah and be close to it. Sometimes, when I was not busy braiding the fringes of his tallit, I used them to kiss the Torah as it was paraded around the congregation. Now, lifting the Torah, I was as close to it as a person could be.

My Bat Mitzvah marked an important milestone for me. I was now counted among the people of Israel and now ready to take on the obligation of becoming a bat mitzvah. Although my grandfather had always said that it wasn't my obligation, I think he would have been thrilled and would have *shept nachas* (felt great pride) from my decision to become a bat mitzvah.

My daughter is now growing up in a congregation where women are active participants in Jewish life. They read Torah, they celebrate B'not Mitzvah, and they wear, if they choose, tallitot. She will never hear that a mitzvah is not her obligation. She will have myriad choices.

**Marcia Bronstein** is a member of Congregation Adath Jeshurun in Elkins Park, Pennsylvania. She is Vice President of Development at the Jewish Community Centers of Greater Philadelphia. She and her husband of twenty years, Eric Salmansohn, have two children, Ross and Lia. Her son bought his Bar Mitzvah tallit last year, a blue and white satin tallit that came with a blue velvet bag. Her daughter Lia will choose her tallit in two years.

# The Curtain of Heaven

## Shoni Evan BenDavid

A man's tallit is his refuge from a world of frustration, confusion, and constant needs. When he puts on his tallit, it is as if he wrapped himself in the curtain of heaven, as if the Creator's wings were protecting him and giving him comfort. In this place of shelter and seclusion, he then prays to G-d for himself and his family.

My grandmother Reva, of blessed memory, gave me a gift on my Bar Mitzvah that it took me another eleven years to truly appreciate. She gave me my tallit. Even though I didn't know what the real significance of that gift was at the time, I cherished it more than any other possession I had ever had. It was my Jewish ID card, the symbol of my grandmother's love—both for me and for being Jewish.

She made the tallit of raw silk on the outside, which she batiked by hand to form the design of the Magen David, the blessing of the tallit, and other artwork that represents our family heritage. The inside was done in smooth silk and was also batiked, but the pattern looked like the night sky in the desert, with more stars than could be counted. It looked like the promise G-d made to Avraham about his descendants being as numerous as the stars in the sky.

Whenever I wore this tallit, I always felt as if I were surrounded by the whole universe. And thanks to the boundless love my grandmother gave me, I felt that I was a bright star in that universe as well.

Much later, when I began to learn Torah for myself, I found that this analogy was no mere coincidence. In the bracha over the tallit, we say that it is a garment stretching out over the heavens like a curtain. The word *curtain* in Hebrew is *careeayh*. This word is similar to one in the Book of Genesis, cited in the verse, "So G-d made a firmament, and separated between the waters which were below the firmament and the waters which were above the firmament. And it was so. G-d called the firmament heaven" (Genesis 1:7–8). The word *careeayh* (curtain) and the word *lirakeeayh* (firmament) both indicate a separator of one world from another. In addition they both have the same numerical value, or Gematriah, of 410. The kabbalistic meaning of that equivalent value is that when we are wrapped in the tallit, we are wrapped in heaven itself.

The tallit my grandma made me held me tight when I was the most alone. And now, when I am in the midst of starting my own family, I am blessed to have it still holding me as tightly as ever, and with as much love, if not more.

The tallit was made with a matching kippah and carrying bag, all of silk and batiked by my grandmother's loving hand. They will be with me always and, with the help of G-d, my son will one day have the same gift handed down to him on his Bar Mitzvah.

So beautiful is this garment—both in sight and in meaning—that it is often referred to as the "rabbinical garb of the World to Come."

**Shoni Evan BenDavid** lives in Jerusalem and is studying to be a rabbi. He has also produced an Israeli TV show called *Ask the Rabbi*, and a documentary for the Israeli Defense Forces.

# A Special Tallit Ritual for Brianna

## Rabbi Amy Small and Ava Schlesinger

*[Editor's Note: This is the transcript of special tallit ritual conducted as part of a Bat Mitzvah ceremony at Congregation Beth Hatikvah in Chatham, New Jersey, a Reconstructionist synagogue.]*

The tallit, or prayer shawl, is a highly respected object. Wearing one is a public declaration of our love and respect for and devotion to Judaism. Today we will have a special ceremony combining this declaration with Brianna's transition from childhood into womanhood. As we do so, Brianna will be encircled by the three living generations of women who are here to protect her, love her, and teach her. At this time we invite Brianna's grandmothers, mother, and aunts— Aunt Laurie, Aunt Judy, Aunt Debby, and Aunt Gayle— and first cousins—Jaime, Alison, and Jennifer—to come stand in a circle in front of the bimah.

The significant parts of a tallit are the tzitziyot (the fringes) attached to the four corners of the rectangular cloth. There are a number of symbolisms attributed to the knots and the windings, but today they will have a special and personal meaning. Brianna, today, each corner of these tallitot will represent the generations of strong women in your family who have accepted the responsibility to guide you and love you as you journey through your life.

I ask that each member of this circle and Brianna take one tzitzit in your left hand. Brianna, today, this fringe on the tallit represents the incredible gift you have been given by your grandmothers. Both of these women have modeled courage. In generations where women often did not have careers outside the home, your grandmothers were both successful in their fields. Grandma Sarah built a business that has grown beyond anyone's wildest dreams, and Grandma Janice returned to college, eventually earning her master's degree, and then dedicated her career to educating children. But even more striking is the tenacity both of your grandmothers had in raising their families. Each in her own way showed her children that they were loved and valuable and could follow any dream of their choosing.

Brianna, your grandmothers have not been shy in pronouncing their love for you. Feel that love as you stand inside this circle today.

Everyone should now take another tzitzit in your hand. This tzitzit symbolizes the fierce love of the mothers in this circle. It is clear that these two families value motherhood in a passionate way. Through thick and thin, the moms in this circle know their obligation and practice their commitment to their children.

Brianna, your mom wants you to know that it is your right to choose whatever kind of life you want for yourself and that she will support you throughout your journey. As you hold this second tzitzit in your hand, take a moment to receive the love of the mothers standing in this circle today and the love of the mothers in this family from three generations.

The third tzitzit, which everyone should now hold, is dedicated to your aunts. What an amazing group: Aunt Laurie, Judy, Debby, and Gayle. The creativity, ambition and love are palpable in this group.

Brianna, it's as if you have a community of mothers to seek guidance from. Each of these special ladies holds you in her heart, enabling you to draw upon her wisdom and love as escorts along the way. Take a moment to hear their wise voices inside you—they are with you always.

Please now hold the final tzitzit. This is dedicated to the youngest generation of women in this family circle. This is your generation, Brianna, and the bond that you have established with your cousins will be an everlasting bond of friendship and love that will carry each of you through the twists and turns of the years to come. Jaime, Alison, Jennifer, and Brianna—your commitment to each other must be binding. With this fourth tzitzit in your hands, promise today that you will be there for each other always, both in spirit and in body.

It is now time to wrap the tallit around your shoulders.

We ask that anybody who has a tallit do the same, as we listen and embrace the following words from the Kabbalah:

I AM HERE enwrapping myself in this fringed robe, in fulfillment of the command of my Creator, as it is written in the Torah, they shall make them a fringe upon the corners of their garments throughout their generations. And even as I cover myself with the tallit in this world, so may my soul deserve to be clothed with a beauteous spiritual robe in the World to Come, in the Garden of Eden.

Derash: The tallit is a "garment of brightness." It links us with the whole universe, with the whole of nature. The blue thread within it reminds us that the heaven and earth can touch, that the elements of our universe are all wondrously connected. (*Kol Haneshamah Shabbat Vehagim*)

בָּרְכִי נַפְשִׁי אֶת יְיָ, יְיָ אֱלֹהַי גָּדַלְתָּ מְּאֹד, הוֹד וְהָדָר לָבָשְׁתָּ. עֹטֶה אוֹר כַּשַּׂלְמָה, נוֹטֶה שָׁמַיִם כַּיְרִיעָה.

*Barhi nafshi et adonay, adonay ehlohai me'od, hod v'hadar lavashta. Oteh or kasalma, noteh shamayim kay'ri'ah.*

Bless, O my soul, THE ONE! ABUNDANT ONE, my God, how great you grow! In majesty and beauty you are dressed, wrapping yourself in light as in a garment, stretching out the heavens like a shawl. (Psalm 104:1–2)

בָּרוּךְ אַתָּה יְיָ אֱלֹהֵינוּ מֶלֶךְ הָעוֹלָם, אֲשֶׁר קִדְּשָׁנוּ בְּמִצְוֹתָיו וְצִוָּנוּ לְהִתְעַטֵּף בַּצִּיצִת.

*Baruh atah adonay eloheynu meleh ha'olam asher kidshanu bemitzvotav vetzivanu lehitatef batzitzit.*

Blessed are You, VEILED ONE, our God, the Sovereign of all worlds, who has made us holy with your mitzvot, and commanded us to wrap ourselves amid the fringed tallit.

מַה יָּקָר חַסְדְּךָ, אֱלֹהִים וּבְנֵי אָדָם בְּצֵל כְּנָפֶיךָ יֶחֱסָיוּן. יִרְוְיֻן מִדֶּשֶׁן בֵּיתֶךָ, וְנַחַל עֲדָנֶיךָ תַשְׁקֵם. כִּי עִמְּךָ מְקוֹר חַיִּים, בְּאוֹרְךָ נִרְאֶה אוֹר. מְשֹׁךְ חַסְדְּךָ לְיֹדְעֶיךָ, וְצִדְקָתְךָ לְיִשְׁרֵי לֵב

*Mah yakar has'd'ha elohim.*

How precious is your love, O God, when earthborn find the shelter of your wing! They're nourished from the riches of your house. Give drink to them from your Edenic stream. For with you is the fountain of all life, in your Light do we behold all light. Extend your love to those who know you, and your justice to those honest in their hearts. (Psalm 36:8–11)

**Rabbi Amy Joy Small** has been the rabbi of Reconstructionist Congregation Beth Hatikvah in Chatham, New Jersey, since 1997. She is currently President of the Reconstructionist Rabbinical Association, chairs the Rabbinic Cabinet of MetroWest, and sits on the Executive Committee of the National UJC Rabbinic Cabinet, the Executive Council of Religions for Peace, and the National Interreligious Leadership Delegation for Peace in the Middle East. Rabbi Small was previously the Rabbi of Temple B'nai Shalom in Benton Harbor, Michigan and B'nai Yisrael Reconstructionist Congregation, in South Bend, Indiana.

**Ava Schlesinger** is a licensed clinical social worker and Director of Terra Sky Center for Wellness in Summit, New Jersey. She lives in Summit and is a member of Congregation Beth Hatikvah.

# Last Letter from My Father

*Frada Sklar Wallach*

My father's tallis—he never called it a tallit—helped me to walk again. My father died in 1992 at the age of ninety-six. It was five years after I had been fired from an executive position in advertising, and I was still in denial that after more than twenty years as an award-winning writer and vice president at Doyle Dane Bernbach, all that I could get was a little freelance work here and there. Not much to keep two children in college and pay the rent. My husband had died when the children were six and eight, and advertising had allowed us to live comfortably, if not lavishly, until now.

After months of no work, and no savings to draw on, I went back to being a secretary, which is where I had started out in what seemed like a lifetime ago. I was lucky enough to get a job as a second secretary to a very important CEO of a large corporation. I made $15 an hour and had full medical benefits. I was grateful. But I was limping badly. Out of the blue, it seemed, I was diagnosed with severe arthritis of my right hip and needed a hip replacement. I checked with Personnel and was told that I could take a leave of absence and and would be fully covered medically. No problem. Just a few days later, also out of the blue, my boss was fired. I was devastated to learn that my job was being eliminated. They would give me four weeks' salary, period. All medical coverage would end the day I left. I was deeply depressed and practically begged the folks in Personnel to see if they couldn't continue my medical coverage for one more month. "We can't do that," they said. "It's impossible."

Forgive me for digressing and talking entirely about myself, when this is all about my father and his tallis. My father was an Orthodox Jew. He belonged to a small synagogue near both of our apartments in Manhattan. Until his mid-nineties, cane in one hand, shopping bags in the other, he walked slowly to shul every morning and evening to help the rabbi. He was called the "Manager," but he had no official function. He bought milk and challah and orange juice and Manischevitz wine for after prayers when the rabbi was running short. He carried his very worn tallis in an equally worn prayer bag whose Hebrew letters, probably once brilliant gold, were now shadowy and unreadable.

One of the most important things to my father was his letter writing. I could never match his gift of writing long, funny or serious, but always moving letters to people he enjoyed, or who could help him or me or my children in some way. He wrote to Christiaan Barnard congratulating him on his first successful heart transplant, to John and Robert Kennedy, to Senator Al D'Amato and Congressman David Green, to Russell Baker, and to Merian C. Cooper, an old Army buddy. He wrote to friends and relatives and, to my embarrassment, to my teachers and to my employer, William Bernbach, telling him how he might get a new account (which he did, thanks to my Dad). He wrote often to the *New York Times*. And he always got answers with thanks and suggestions and warm wishes and personal signatures. I've saved the carbon copies of most of his letters: Maybe one day I'll publish them. But that's another story.

MY FATHER HAD no formal education, except for *cheder*. He had to leave school very early to help support a brother and three sisters. When people later in life asked where he had been educated, he always told them it was the school of hard knocks. That, and reading the *New*

*York Times* every day. He was eloquent, almost poetic, in all his writing.

So, back to the tallis. It was my last week at work and I was in great pain and trying to do more sitting than standing. With not much concern for this, I was called into my boss' office and asked if I could deliver a package to Merrill Lynch for him. It had to be personally signed for and returned. He said I could use the company limousine, and I agreed. When I got to the street, a tall friendly driver opened the door of a long wine-colored limo. He helped me in and I slowly slid into a comfortable position. My hand touched something soft and bulky, and I picked it up to look at it. It was an incredibly beautiful prayer bag, not at all like my father's. It was larger and had Hebrew letters embroidered in gold, shining, as they never had from my father's worn bag. "Somebody left their prayer bag," I told the driver. It was surprising to me because the corporation I worked for had a mere smattering of Jewish employees, possibly a few hundred out of many thousands.

"Oh, that's Mr. Moscowitz's," the driver said.

"Saul Moscowitz? The President's? You're kidding!"

"No. I take him to synagogue every morning before work. Right here." We were passing a small, unpretentious building as he spoke.

"The one where Rabbi Seesa officiates?" I asked in disbelief.

"That's the one," he said.

It was the shul where my father had prayed each day for thirty years, where both of my children had been given their Hebrew names at birth, where my marriage had been blessed, celebrated and presided over by Rabbi Seesa.

As I rode in a state of shakiness and unreality to my destination and back, I asked myself, "What would my father have done?" Of course, I knew what he would have done. He would have written a letter. He would write to Mr. Moscowitz telling him about me and my need for medical insurance and of finding, of all things, his prayer bag, and asking if, by some chance, he had known my father, the "Manager."

I got back to the office and turned on my computer. It seemed wrong. My father had always written his letters on an old Royal typewriter, and I felt I should run home and write this letter—which was obviously being guided by my father's hand—on anything but a computer. But I had to use my computer.

My letter to Mr. Moscowitz was a good one. I was my father's daughter.

I wrote about finding his prayer bag on my errand, of the possibility that maybe he knew my father, the shul "Manager," of my situation and my feeling that this was divine intervention. I asked if there was anything he could do to extend my health coverage for a mere month, and told him what it would mean to me. I sent the letter in the hand-delivered interoffice mail, and waited. A day. Two days. Four days. I checked with his secretary to make sure the president was in town that week. He was. If my father had written this letter, it would have gotten a reply. Presidents of countries and companies answered him, signing their own names and adding their comments in handwritten asides. I lost the little faith I had left in my writing.

THE DAY I had to leave my job I went to Personnel to sign a job elimination package. With a slightly puzzled expression, a clerk checked a page twice before telling me, "You'll receive a severance check for one month and continued medical coverage for the next six months."

"What?" I stammered.

"We received a memo from Saul Moscowitz. He didn't say why. It's highly unusual, but he wants you to have full coverage. Would you like to read this and sign it?"

My father had channeled one of his best letters yet. He was my *gutta betta* (go-between), able to speak to the highest power in my behalf. My children thought this an enormous and fortuitous coincidence. It wasn't. His prayer bag and worn tallis were all the proof I needed of a miracle.

**Frada Sklar Wallach** lives in Manhattan. She has two grown children and is grandma to Isabella and Rachel, with another on the way. She was a Senior Copywriter and Vice President at the advertising agency of Doyle Dane Bernbach, and won many awards there, including an Emmy nomination for a thirty-minute film documentary for the Federation of Jewish Philanthropies, called "Bridge Over Troubled Waters," with Jack Guilford. She is presently at work on children's books and an autobiographical short story, and is a member of Central Synagogue in Manhattan.

# A Beloved Father's Tallit

*Sheldon Scholl*

By 1967, my father Max had retired from the garment industry and was living in Long Branch, New Jersey. He had been born in Roumania, and in 1912, as a teenager, had immigrated with his parents and his brothers and sisters to the United States—part of the great wave of Jewish immigration in the early years of the twentieth century. He had attended school in this country for about two years and then had gone to work in a factory in the garment district of New York.

My father was self-taught, and enjoyed reading anything and everything, including my textbooks throughout my school years. Unfortunately, without a formal education, his job opportunities were limited and his final job was as a production manager in the garment trades.

Even though he had a bad heart, he and my mother enjoyed visiting us in upstate New York, where my family lived, and spending time with their grandsons. Travel meant taking the bus and the train, or my driving them back and forth from their home to New Jersey. Yet taking mass transit was no chore for them, just as driving was no chore for me. We reveled in each other's company.

In June 1967, while visiting us in Carmel, New York, he suffered a series of heart attacks. The first one occurred in the doctor's office, the second in the ambulance, and the third and fatal one occurred in the hospital. He had promised my mother that he would not die on her birthday, but he did pass away the following day.

Now to the story of the tallit.

My father did not have his tallit with him when he passed away, and this posed a problem. From the hospital he was transferred to a funeral home for burial in the Old Montifiore Cemetery in Queens, New York. I decided that I would have him buried in my tallit, which I had received on my wedding day in April 1951.

After the shiva (the seven-day mourning period) was over, I returned with my mother to her home in Long Branch, where I found my father's tallit. Since then, I have worn my father's tallit whenever I attend services. At present I am a trustee of Temple Har Zion in Mount Holly, New Jersey, having moved to the Garden State.

Though there are more costly tallitot worn by many congregants, I am indeed proud to wear a tallit worn by my father for over sixty years. Someday, when I die, I will be buried in my father's tallit.

**Sheldon Scholl**, who lives in Columbus, New Jersey, is a retired high school counselor-psychologist. He is a member of the Board of Trustees of Temple Har Zion.

# Tallit Traditions

### Rabbi Edward Goldstein

On January 3, 1966, my grandfather, Sam Goldstein, of blessed memory, was rushed to Massachusetts General Hospital after a three-day flu. He had long suffered from congestive heart failure. We received word later that evening that he had passed away.

My father called the undertaker and the Bostoner rebbe, and preparations for his funeral were under way. Early the next morning my father received a phone call from the *Chevra Kadisha* (Burial Society) that my grandfather's silk tallit, bought just a year earlier for my Bar Mitzvah, was unsuitable for a man of his stature and contributions to the community. They were replacing it with a woolen one.

In the decades after World War II, my grandfather and his son, my father, had done electrical work for the Bostoner rebbe's father, R. Pinchas Dovid Horowitz, z"l, in the old West End neighborhood of Boston. They'd also done wiring and other electrical projects for many families and shuls in the then-burgeoning areas of Roxbury, Dorchester, and Mattapan (and later in Brookline and Newton, as well)—much of it gratis. So my grandfather was a well-known and beloved man throughout most of metropolitan Boston.

I encountered one of these rabbis' children when I went to buy my son (now twenty-five) a tallit for his Bar Mitzvah. We went to Ziontalis to choose a tallit and order a custom atarah, with his name embroidered in green (his next younger brother received one in blue nine years later). As we completed the purchases, I commented to my son that this experience reminded me of the time when that same grandfather took me to Davidson's Hebrew Book Store in Dorchester for my tallit and tefillin. The man behind the counter looked surprised and said, "Where?!"

I repeated the store name.

He told me that his father was the rabbi of the Lawrence Avenue shul. I asked if he remembered the electrician with the cane.

"Sure," he replied.

"Well," I said, "that is his great-grandson" whom you just provided with a tallit.

Apropos of my grandfather's woolen tallit, which he never saw: For my father's birthday the following February, my father, now also of blessed memory (1993), had an odd request: He, too, wanted a woolen tallit like the one "Pa was buried in." He davened in that tallit the rest of his life.

WHEN I WAS getting married, my wife purchased for me a white tallit, with a silver atarah on blue velvet. She specifically ordered five rows. She purchased it from Abe Gross, obm, at the House of Israel (then on Queens Boulevard). When we came in a few weeks later, Mr. Gross was embarrassed to show us five rows of silver on blue satin—not velvet. My then-fiancée, Michele Goodman, informed him that that was not what she had ordered. He told us he knew that, but figured he'd see if we would accept it. A few weeks later, he called us again. The atarah was in. We came to the store and he put it on the counter. I started laughing uncontrollably, and he joined in. For a minute or so, Michele did not realize that there were six rows of silver on velvet. The last row was his gift. Mr. Gross was a mensch among men.

A quarter-century later, when our daughter became a *kallah* (bride), I took my then–future son-in-law to Judaica Plus to purchase a tallit for him. I told him and Aaron Goldstein (no relation, though we call each other "cousin"), the story of my silver atarah. He promptly took the price of one row of silver off the bill (partially at my son-in-law's suggestion), commenting that it was—now a family tradition!

AS A RABBI, I have recognized and elevated the role the tallit plays in synagogue life. It was the custom of Rabbi Manuel Saltzman, obm, of Congregation Kehillath Israel in Brookline to wear a thin little silk prayer scarf (as I call it) over his rabbinical robes on Simchat Torah. A sort of Purim joke, I always imagined. I have always used the tallit as a chuppah on Simchat Torah for the *hatanim* (bridegrooms), at aufrufs, and at fiftieth-anniversary celebrations.

PERSONALLY, OVER THE last few years, I have adopted the Bostoner (and Orthodox) custom of wearing my tallit over my head during *tefillah* (prayer), leaving it on until after *Kedusha*. I began when my mother had her heart surgery and the rebbe asked me to be *shliach tzibbur* (reader) that morning as a way to accelerate her *refuah* (recovery), I presume. As an aside, I was hesitant about doing so, since only an *aveil* (mourner) usually davens as *shatz* (reader), but my doubts were calmed when the rebbe asked me, "Eddie, what's the matter? You don't know how?"

Of course, I had a rejoinder: "No, Rebbe. I know how. It cost my father lots of money for me to learn."

**Rabbi Edward Goldstein** is a 1978 graduate of the Jewish Theological Seminary and has served pulpits in Brooklyn, Queens, and Nassau County, most recently in Jackson Heights. He is a Bostoner chasid and a graduate of the Maimonides School in Brookline, Massachusetts. He and his wife, the former Michele Goodman, are the parents of five children (two married). He has also served as Past Master of his Masonic Lodge.

# The Cavaricci Tallit

## Rabbi Joel Soffin

When my son was preparing for his Bar Mitzvah, we went to buy him a suit. While we were in the store, he noticed a pair of Cavaricci pants on sale. It didn't matter to him that the color was an unappealing shade of green or that it was two sizes too big. The price was right, and he wanted to buy it. Unable to deal with such a purchase, I waited in the car while his mother negotiated the deal with the salesperson.

A few minutes later, my son came out with tears in his eyes. He had misread the price, and it was, in fact, too expensive for him. Why did he want these Cavaricci pants so badly? Was everyone else wearing them? No. Were they particularly fashionable? No. When I explained that he was, unfortunately, the son of a father who would never buy such pants for himself, he said, "But Dad, I need them."

Need them? That I could understand. So the next day I bought Cavaricci pants for him in black in the correct size.

Soon it was time to select his tallit. None of the dozens in our synagogue's Judaica shop appealed to him. Neither did any in the store on the Lower East Side, which he dismissed with a wave of his hand after a ten-second perusal of the hundreds of choices. Not even the salesman's desperate run after us with side curls aflutter could change his mind.

Then he saw it in a corner of a nearby store. It had probably sat in that window in its dried-out plastic tallit bag for twenty-five years. This was the tallit of his dreams. Why? It had a green stripe, and green meant the New York Jets!

I refused to buy that tallit for him, but agreed that the one we would purchase would indeed have such a green stripe. Before we could locate a green-striped tallit, however, I came across a weaver who permitted members of the family to weave part of the tallit themselves. All of us, including my son's grandparents, would go to her workshop, and there would be a green stripe in the finished prayer shawl. Suddenly, my son wasn't interested in this expedition. He refused to go and wanted to have nothing to do with a family-made tallit.

"Why did I want him to have that particular tallit?" he asked. "Was everyone making such a tallit for their sons?"

No.

"Would it be especially fashionable?"

No.

When my son was ready to declare that the discussion was over, I said three words to him that made all the difference: "I need it."

He agreed immediately and on his Bar Mitzvah day, he wore the tallit his proud family had helped to weave for him.

**Joel Soffin** received ordination from the Hebrew Union College–Jewish Institute of Religion in New York in 1976. He has served as spiritual leader of Temple Shalom in Succasunna, New Jersey, for more than twenty-five years. He now enjoys wearing a large, bright tallit, which was woven by Ethiopian Jews in Ethiopia.

# Rebel Without a Shawl

### H. Lewis Stone

When you are fourteen, the world is not exactly your oyster.

Being a Jewish teenager in the 1970s was no different than it is today. You try to make a statement, to develop your own style—a style distinctly different from that of your parents. Yet, as Conservative Jews, my friends and I needed to remain within the confines of socially acceptable behavior.

Our local USY (United Synagogue Youth) chapter in Fair Lawn, New Jersey, sponsored a tallit-making project, and a group of us decided to make ours in brightly colored fabrics. We all sat together in shul, in the back on the left, so even friends who were casual worshipers could easily find us.

Rich "Winna" Trietman (he had a girlfriend from Queens who thought he was a Winner) made a blue one. Norman "Beaver" Meyerowitz (his father was a furrier and he had buck teeth as a kid) made a red one. Marc Haar made a red, white, and blue–striped tallit with an atarah of stars. I made a yellow tallit with brown corners. Sitting together, we called ourselves the Color Guard.

At a time when few tallitot were anything but white with blue or white with black, just about the only thing you could do to make your tallit distinctive was to add gold or silver trim. When we arrived on the scene with our multicolored prayer shawls, most congregants thought our color choices were beyond the pale. Older women would stop the rabbi in his tracks and say, "This cannot be kosher!" They were astonished when the rabbi said there was nothing wrong with it. They just shook their heads in dismay, amazed at what the world was coming to.

Here, in the arena of tallit law, we knew more than the adults and this knowledge was validated by none other than the rabbi. It knocked the old guard off kilter. A popular expression of the day was "Question Authority," and that is exactly what we were doing. I remember an older man stopping me and checking my tzitit, hoping to find a mistake, and then shaking his head as he walked away, his mission not accomplished.

Acceptance came slowly. One day the president of the shul said about Marc's red, white, and blue tallit: "I don't know whether he should bless it or salute it."

By creating our own exclusive club, we defined ourselves as observant Jews, but on own terms. Our polychromatic tallitot forced the older generation to widen their view of acceptable Jewish practice, while wearing them gave us credibility as young adults capable of researching and executing a project with conviction. We became Rebels With a Cause.

Most of us have gone on to successful careers and remain committed Jews to this day. I credit part of our success to having mastered the art of working within the system (wearing tallitot) yet establishing ourselves as individuals (making those tallitot distinctly our own). Most of all, I think my own teenage act of courage taught me to be a better parent now that my own son is a teenager.

**H. Lewis Stone**, with wife Julie and sons Jeremy and Jonathan, lives in Morris Township, New Jersey. After spending twenty years in trust banking, Mr. Stone started his own consulting firm specializing in municipal finance. He is also president of a firm specializing in the liquidation of estates and trust collectibles using the eBay auction site. He is a member of Morristown Jewish Center–Beit Yisrael and serves on the House/Building Committee.

# Papa's Tallit

## *Anne Krasner*

Sometimes one person's tallit figures prominently in the life-cycle event of someone else, as my father's tallit did for my best friend Jenny Segal. The events I'm about to chronicle occurred long ago, just after World War II, when marriage was the dream of all women of marriageable age and beyond.

At that time, my friend Jenny had been a schoolteacher but she'd changed careers to become a member of the Hillel Foundation of New York University. She was also an excellent tennis player. But dates with young men were scarce. Finally, she met the man of her dreams. His name was Sid.

My father was known as "Papa" to all my friends. Jenny brought her boyfriend to meet Papa as though he were her father, too. Jenny's father had died when she was young. She lived with her mother and a sister who was a schoolteacher and had married a teacher. They had no children. The whole family was poor.

Jenny had hoped and prayed for Sid to propose, and one day he did. The next morning she called me at work—I was the secretary to the editor of *Parents* magazine. The phone rang just as I walked in. Jenny said excitedly, "Anne, Sid proposed last night and we're getting married today." She then said, "Anne, I want you to bring Papa's tallit to the Hillel Foundation. The tallit will serve as a chuppah. You and my sister and her husband and Sid are the only ones who are going to be here." (As it turned out, another friend and Sid's sister also joined in the happy ceremony.)

I was shocked at her request but very happy. Yet how could I leave the office—I had just arrived?!

I went to the editor, Mrs. Littledale, and nervously asked her if I could be excused because my best friend was going to be married. She said, "Go right now." It was a great day for all of us.

I took the subway from New York back home to Brooklyn, picked up Papa's tallit, and decided to bring refreshments. I shopped for wine and cake.

When I arrived at Hillel, I went from room to room to collect four window poles. I tied the four corners of the tallit to the poles in order to make a very special chuppah. The Hillel rabbi performed the ceremony. Four of us—another friend, Jenny's sister, Sid's sister, and I— held the four poles on which the chuppah was raised. It was a wonderful and happy wedding, followed by the kiddush that I had supplied.

After her first son was born, she had two more sons. And each son was taught the story of the tallit.

I took the tallit back to my Papa's home. Today, I still have it. My fondest memory of that tallit will always be its role in that one, wonderful day, when my best friend got married. The tallit encompasses my family history within its folds, as it was passed down to me from my father, and to him from his. (My father was buried in a separate tallit.) But this tallit is also a symbol of Jewish friendship, an enduring bond between two Jewish girls looking for love and happiness in the New World.

**Anne Krasner**, now over ninety years old and living in Hewlett, Long Island, attends the Five Town Senior Center in Woodmere, New York, where she teaches Yiddish. She also takes writing classes, and this story grew out of a recent writing assignment.

# Weddings and Wilderness

## Dave Bean

T he darkest secret of my Jewish past is that I was never Bar Mitzvahed. I started my Hebrew studies a year late, and then I couldn't see my way around learning disabilities to master Hebrew. But when my younger brother, Jonathan, was old enough for religious training, I told him he had to do it for himself and for me.

So now when I hold his tallit, all creamy off-white with brown, black, red, orange, yellow, green, blue, and maroon stripes, I don't just think of it as his. I imagine that it is somehow "ours." The corner tassels, the tzitzit, are reinforced with silver embroidery. The strip down the edge says in Hebrew: "Because we are of Zion we have been given the Torah."

Until I was married I ceded all things Jewish to my brother, Jonathan. He'd been a bar mitzvah. He'd decided as a teenager that our Reform congregation wasn't Jewish enough for him, so each week he attended a Conservative synagogue with a friend instead. He'd spent summers leading tours in Israel while I skied Vermont, Argentina, and Utah. When I asked to use his tallit for our wedding, he readily agreed, but that's just the beginning of the story.

I PLAY OUT the fixed rope, watching it settle fifty feet short of the canyon bottom, all sand against a lazy tributary of the Escalante River. Nothing can temper what this woman, soon to become my mother-in-law, will say. I show her the Anazai chipped sandstone Moki Steps, explain how on steep sandstone your shoes should fully

press the sugary rock. She takes a tentative step, grip-
ping the rope as if the end were directly connected to her
New Jersey home. The day is all heat with a dazzle of
sunshine. And in the midst of a desperate side step,
Judy—my mother-in-law-to-be—tells me I'm crazy if I
think she'll allow her younger son or daughter to go
down into this canyon.

Until then the Gulch was where Brooke and I
planned to be married on the first full moon in August,
a three-mile unmarked hike at the end of a fifty-mile dirt
two-track. For us it is a sacred spot, our wedding a
sacred ceremony. The logic of linking the two ran out
quicker than our rope.

Our wedding began as a shared dream first spoken
beneath the harvest moon at a wild party of friends and
family in an equally wild place. The wedding invitations
had been mailed out long before. It was early spring and
every chance we could, Brooke and I scouted potential
desert wedding sites after Judy nixed the Gulch. Over
fifty people had RSVPed, even though the only clue
about the wedding's location was a palm-sized, photo-
copied map with an X to mark the now-cancelled Gulch site.

Over dinner at Hanukkah my parents, who were in
their sixties, had said they'd go anywhere Brooke and I
chose for the wedding. They had assured us that whatever we felt, they'd feel. We had their blessing, but we
also had their lives in our hands, along with seventy others. More RSVPs arrived daily.

Hours later, driving up out of the desert, Brooke and
I performed some sort of crazy consolation ritual, and
then decided to be married at Lower Calf Creek Falls. At
first it seemed absurd to choose a desert place almost as
tame as a national park. Lower Calf Creek Falls is a
Bureau of Land Management campground, featured on
postcards, calendars, even in a *New York Times* travel
article. The 126-foot waterfall is located at the end of a
2.8-mile interpretive trail that shadows the creek. There
is a gray-blue brochure with numbered signs explaining
all about buffalo berries and pictographs, cryptogamic
soil and lizards. Stones and logs mark the edge of the
trail. No cliffs, no slick rock, no problem.

The week before we were married, Brooke and I

finally sat down to rewrite our rabbi's wedding ceremony. We made sure our sisters and brother and parents each had a part. As we wrote, we imagined the desert of the Talmud, trying to write ourselves back in time.

The wedding procession was all drums and bare feet. Almost everyone wore a specially embroidered full moon baseball cap given out at the trailhead as protection against sunstroke.

When I first met Judy, and she struggled with the idea of seeing her daughter married in the desert, I assured her that it never rains in August in the desert. It had been a rainless spring, the summer drier still. But as the ceremony came to a close, a wind came up and caught my brother's multicolored tallit, untying it from one of the four-cottonwood saplings and our hiking rabbi looked questioningly skyward. It was as if that prayer shawl had a mind of its own and could take flight up past the waterfall, beyond the steep canyon walls.

After I smashed the ceremonial glass, it rained—not long, but hard enough to leave no doubt. People said the rain ensured Brooke's fertility. And maybe they were right. We have three healthy children—two girls and a boy. In *River Notes*, Barry Lopez writes that, "Before we could ask for rain there had to be someone to do something completely selfless, with no hope for success."

Brooke and I were the last ones to hike out, meandering along the sandy dirt path by Calf Creek, savoring the light fading into the sandstone canyon walls, avoiding the others, trying not to hear their laughter. But I knew how elusive a dream given voice under a full moon is. It might take a lifetime of staring up at that full moon, the tallit we sheltered under, and all we believe about the most vacant stretches of land to reconcile the wild inconsistencies of life.

In the end, Jonathan's tallit bore the hope that sheltered our union and finally conveyed all we imagined. We could follow Calf Creek almost till the end of time, our own wild turn of the mind past the rings and ritual, the tallit, the toasts, and the champagne, the finality of our one-word vow: "*L'olam.*"

**Dave Bean** teaches English and history at Gould Academy in Bethel, Maine.

# Mom's Tallit

### Farrell Bloch

[Editor's Note: This poignant story is a work of fiction, unlike the other pieces in this collection.]

David's deepening commitment to Jewish observance suggested graduation from his shul's racks of tallitot. With the Chanukah gelt from his mother, David purchased a new tallit, the first time he'd celebrated Chanukah with an overtly Jewish gift. Mom, you bought me a tallis, he reported, replacing the in-vogue Sephardic *t* with the Ashkenazic *s* more familiar to her.

Elderly and immobile, David's mother likely would never visit a synagogue again. Only via the tallit would she attend shul with her son. The last garment David's mother supplied him, the tallit ended a wardrobe chain that had expanded in number, clothing size, and variety; and spanned diapers, school clothes laid out for the next morning, and mounds of college laundry.

When his mother became seriously ill, David recited her Hebrew name during the *M'sheberach* prayer each Shabbat, clutching his tallit fringes tight, as if his grip could transfer strength to her frailty. As vigor deserted her ailing body, David's prayers became a plea for more time.

After his mother passed away, David recited kaddish weekday mornings at *Shacharit* services and twilights at *Mincha-Maariv*. Now in daily use, his tallit aged rapidly, its pristine white fading like teeth over a lifetime, its once-sharp creases flabby like deteriorating muscles.

Mom, you bought me a tallis comforted David. He'd use this tallit for the rest of his life, like the elderly men at shul who still wore the full-sized tallitot that had wrapped them luxuriantly at their B'nai Mitzvah.

ATTENDING WEEKDAY SERVICES occasionally after his mourning period, David stored his tallit in the small daily minyan chapel, after extending it on the chapel's table for proper folding. Following services one Shabbat, as David doubled his tallit in halves, then in quarters, he felt dampness. Had it rained during services, and had someone left a window open? Did the ceiling leak?

David swept his tallit from the table. Inspecting it, he discovered an elliptical brownish blot. He smelled the unmistakable aroma of scotch. Each Shabbat a few worshippers left services before the weekly announcements and chanting of *Adon Olam* to celebrate Shabbat with *a bisil schnapps*. This week they'd been careless, spilling scotch on the chapel table and not wiping it up.

David unfurled his tallit and draped it over the back of three chairs. What could he do about the spot? He'd always called his mother when tomato or chocolate invaded cotton or wool, and applied her remedies of seltzer or baking soda. What could he do now other than keep his tallit away from the wet table? At shul, water was his only cleaning product. But no one brought a tallit into the bathroom or ran it under the water cooler.

Elderly congregants rarely cleaned their tallitot, tributes to decades of prayer. Centuries earlier, when rabbis wore their tallitot at Friday night dinner, the voluble Rav Levi Yitzhak of Berditchev had visited the calmer Rav Baruch of Medzhibozh, grandson of the Baal Shem Tov. In an enthusiastic proclamation of love for the Almighty, Rav Levi Yitzhak had thrown a plate of fish into the air, staining Rav Baruch's tallit. Rav Baruch regarded the blemish as a badge of honor, a reminder of Rav Levi Yitzhak's *kavanah*, his enthusiasm and devotion. But the stain on David's tallit commemorated inconsiderate congregants, not a pious rabbi.

Take the tallit to a dry cleaner? Not on Shabbat: That would be violating the prohibition against shopping.

Maybe during the week. But which cleaner? A congregant might know. But a well-meaning dry cleaner might loosen the fringes, or worse, defile the tallit permanently by piercing it with a tagged safety pin. Even thinking about commerce was improper for Shabbat. And, not having eaten anything before services, David was hungry. He checked the time. How much kiddush food remained? David tucked his flattened tallit into its bag and left it in the chapel's cabinet. He hurried to the kiddush.

DAVID TOSSED IN bed, hours before dawn. Why hadn't he taken his tallit home and spread it on his bed or table, letting it heal in the secure atmosphere of his house, perhaps basking near a sunny window? If that didn't help, at least—like the proverbial elderly lady's chicken soup brought to the victim of a car accident—it couldn't hurt. Did packing his tallit in its bag overnight worsen the discoloration? Would he have to see the blot he remembered from yesterday—or a much larger one—for the rest of his life?

Should he have invoked the Shabbat provision for emergencies and taken the tallit to a dry cleaner? Because he wouldn't be paying anything until he picked up the cleaned garment, the drop-off might not be classified as shopping. No rabbi would accept that flimsy argument, David realized. And wouldn't a worker's untying the fringes or applying stickers or safety pins be more likely on Shabbat, because of the extra flow of customers and part-time Saturday help, or as a fundamental judgment in response to David's Shabbat violation? Then he'd have to buy another tallit, and no longer be blessed in shul with the remnant of his mother's presence. Were his only choices a new tallit or a stained old one?

DAVID RUSHED TO shul an hour before Sunday *Shacharit* services. He berated himself for his carelessness in not inspecting the table before putting his tallit away, and for his fastidiousness in refusing to fold his tallit at his seat; for his lack of foresight in leaving his tallit to stew overnight in the scotch juices, and for his moral weakness in deserting his tallit while he fed his hungry stomach.

As soon as he arrived, David checked the daily chapel table. Now perfectly dry. With trepidation he unzipped his tallit bag. No waft of liquor assailed his nose; the scotch apparently had dried overnight. David unrolled his tallit, turned it up and to the side, then reversed it. No obvious blemish! He presented his tallit to the window's morning light and inspected each square inch. Not a drop of Shabbat scotch remained!

David slumped into a chair, clutching his tallit to his chest, burying his face in it, then springing up, so that his tearing eyes would not leave a spot. After reciting *l'hitatayf b'tzitzit*, he donned his tallit, wrapping it around his head for a full minute before letting it rest on his shoulders. David danced around the small chapel, skipped to the Shabbat sanctuary, meandered through its empty rows, then strode around the shul. Twenty minutes later, when other worshippers arrived, David returned to the chapel and donned his tefillin.

**Farrell Bloch** is the author of the Jewish-themed novel *Michael's Inheritance*. An economist, he has been an economic and statistical consultant to corporations and government agencies, a frequent expert witness, an assistant professor of economics at Princeton, and an adjunct professor at Georgetown, Johns Hopkins, and the University of Maryland. He lives in Washington, D.C.

# I Gave My Mother a Tallit for Her Birthday

*Beth Levin*

I gave my mother a tallit for her birthday
it was soft and white and simple
made in Israel
with some sparkling threads
woven within

I gave my mother a tallit for her birthday
to honor her learning and teaching and study
her devotion
and commitment
to the Jewish people

I gave my mother a tallit for her birthday
her holy, sparkling, shining light
surrounding her like a cloud
resting gently on the strength
of her shoulders

**Beth Levin** serves as Spiritual Life Educator, combining cantorial and family education duties, at Temple Shir Tikvah in Winchester, Massachusetts.

# A Tallit
# That Still
# Speaks to Me

*Harold Kalter*

"Use this closet in my apartment as your own, my dear Marilyn," Uncle Schweitzer said to my fiancée in his soft, gentle voice. This was my first sign of his generosity.

Uncle Schweitzer was introduced to me when I became engaged to Marilyn. He was an octogenarian then and he was known as a near-blind pious Jew by all the people on University Avenue in the Bronx. Rarely was his first name used.

Most mornings, at 7:00 a.m., he could be seen walking toward Burnside Avenue where his small shul held daily services. Using a large cane with a metal tip, he cleverly maneuvered his way through the streets. Amazingly, in all kinds of weather, he could be seen making this trip to be counted in the minyan.

Beneath his clean jacket was an almost nondescript tallit. His tallit was rather long, and somewhat faded. A tear, caused by wear, had appeared in the center, just below the Hebrew blessing for donning this garment.

Uncle Schweitzer wore this garment proudly, relying on it as a warmer both physically and spiritually.

In heavily accented English, he modestly spoke of the joys in his life. He had a son, twin daughters, and had lived a happy, full life with a loving wife, who was now deceased. Uncle Schweitzer had the comfort of

knowing that Mollie, his wife's sister, was fully committed to helping him through his daily chores and that he
never had to ask directly for anything. He appeared
daily in Mollie's kitchen, where he assumed the responsibility for removing the garbage bag and disposing of it
in the floor's incinerator.

The tzitzit of his tallit never dangled about because
they were tucked neatly in his trousers, held firmly by a
belt and suspenders.

There was always a unique glow in Uncle
Schweitzer's bodily features. When I saw him, I immediately felt at peace with myself. He seemed to emit
warmth, kindness, and an aura of hopefulness. I felt that,
for me, today and tomorrow would be a little bit better
than before I had seen him.

Once, I asked him how he managed to remain so
peaceful. He pointed a finger above and then with an
open hand he touched beneath his shirt revealing a view
of his fading tallit.

In 1967, Uncle Schweitzer died. His funeral was very
simple and attended by almost a hundred people who
came to pay their respects to this remarkable man.

After the *Shloshim* (thirty-day formal mourning period) was over, my mother-in-law, Mollie, asked us to
assist in disposing of much of the apartment's belongings. It was then I was given his tallit. Now, forty years
later, I still put it on almost daily. And I still feel Uncle
Schweitzer's presence. When I envelop myself in this
special piece of cloth, I too feel and experience his special warmth. This warmth makes me feel closer to the
Divine, and, at times, I too believe today and tomorrow
will be better.

**Harold Kalter**, who lives in North Valley Stream, New York, has been
a language arts teacher, an assistant principal, and a certified religious school teacher. He lectures at senior citizens' centers on top-
ics ranging from the Bible as Literature to Old Testament Rituals &
Lore, and does poetry readings for spiritual awakening.

# The Flea Market Tallit

*Patricia Ann Wilson Reber*

I spent many wonderful hours with my Uncle Sidney and Aunt Rita. He always made us laugh, and he had an extremely kind heart. Aunt Rita and he retired and moved out of New York City to a lovely shore community in southern New Jersey. When Uncle Sidney died, we were all so sad. The laughter we once shared with him was permanently silent. Aunt Rita never recovered after he died. Uncle Sid was her balance and her reason for living.

Aunt Rita decided to move closer to the nephew she had grown up with. I believe this was her way of bringing closure to her life with Uncle Sidney. As my husband Bob and I were visiting her to say good-bye, she said to me, "If there is anything here you want, just take it."

I saw an old tallit and said, "Was this Uncle Sid's?"

She said, "No."

This tallit just stared at me. I could tell it had once been stark white, with piercing black stripes. From age and wear, it was now a dark ivory, the black stripes, which had once been vibrant, were now faded and tired. I wondered where this tallit had been and how it had ended up in Ventnor, New Jersey, with Aunt Rita and Uncle Sidney.

The story went that she and Uncle Sid had been at a flea market and had seen it lying on the ground in one man's booth. She had said to vendor, "What are you going to do with that?"

He responded, "That rag? I'm just going to throw it away."

At that point Aunt Rita realized that he had no idea what it was. She said, "How much do you want for it?"

He said, "Lady, just take it." So Aunt Rita took this wonderful piece of history. She brought it home, had it cleaned, and put it away.

I froze for a moment and wondered where this tallit had been. Who had worn this precious prayer shawl years ago? Who had found spiritual solace in its folds? And who would wear it in years to come? These answers I did not know.

I realized, with horror, that all this history could have ended up in a garbage dump. In my mind, this tallit had found a pair of angels in my aunt and uncle.

Much as my aunt had done, I took this piece of history home. I had it cleaned and put it away. Much like my aunt, years later as I was cleaning out a drawer, I came across this tallit, whose history was still a mystery, and which yearned for a new meaning in life. So I decided to create a new history for this orphaned tallit. I did not know how or where or when I would do this. I just knew it would come to me.

Then one day all the pieces fell into place. Our son Matthew, a religion major, is attending his sophomore year of college in Israel. I shared the story of the tallit with him. I asked him to take this tallit to Israel, to keep it close, and to give this wonderful piece of history a new beginning.

He thought that was a lovely idea. He will wear it in prayer. I can't help but think that he will also reflect on the story of the tallit's fortuitous rescue as he wears it. Much like our ancestors who wandered in the desert for forty years, it seems that this tallit has wandered the world as well. Matthew will infuse new meaning—and a future—into this tallit that had survived through the grace of G-d.

**Patricia Ann Wilson Reber** grew up in Florham Park, New Jersey. She currently lives in Chester, New Jersey, with her husband of thirty years. A certified assisted living administrator, she has two grown sons, Bryan, 26, and Matthew, 20. The Rebers belong to Temple Shalom in Succasunna, New Jersey.

# Tallit Links

## Helen Ray Gelman Rib

Our original plan was to return to Maryland in February so that we could be home for a few weeks before flying to Oklahoma for our youngest granddaughter's Bat Mitzvah. All of our children, grandchildren, and close relatives were going to celebrate the simcha. We were really looking forward to the Grand Event.

We had been spending the winter in Arizona with one of our daughters and her family. We had a great time. We visited our California son and his family, went to an Elderhostel, enjoyed the senior activities and gym at the Arizona JCC, and, of course, loved being with the grandkids.

Then my back folded like a house of cards. I caught pneumonia (again) and coughed violently while in a peculiar position. I felt a twinge in my lower back. Within two days I could not walk, sit, stand up, lie down, or move without extreme pain. The MRIs and X-rays showed problems I never even knew I had—scoliosis, mismatched discs, pinched nerves, old scars from an unknown crack in the pelvis, and other diagnoses I still don't understand.

My five days in the hospital passed in a drugged haze. Every moment of the ten days I spent in the rehabilitation center was jam-packed, so I could learn how to walk and use my body again. There were three to four exercise sessions each day. Therapy sessions continued on an outpatient basis when I was discharged. Progress was painfully slow, no matter how hard I tried.

It soon became clear that I should not cram myself into an airplane any time soon. We would have to stay in Arizona until Bat Mitzvah time. It would give my body an extra month of recuperation. We could travel directly to Oklahoma for the festivities.

The next question was clothing. We had brought the right outfits for our Southwest activities, including synagogue attire for Arizona. However, as grandparents of the bat mitzvah, we needed a step or two up in ensemble.

And, I wanted our tallitot. The synagogue in Oklahoma did not require a tallit and did not have any available for congregants. If people wanted to wear one, they supplied their own. Well, we wanted to wear ours. To me, the tallit is a uniform for Jewish morning service. When I don my tallit, I feel ready for prayer. Fingering the tzitzit gives me comfort. Seeing fellow congregants similarly covered with prayer shawls lends a wonderful aura to the service.

My tallit had been creatively crocheted for me by my late mother. My husband's was a beautiful, brand-new one that I had bought for him in honor of our fiftieth wedding anniversary. Even though I am not an accomplished seamstress, I had sewn a tallit for our granddaughter. It was not an artistic or complicated creation, but it turned out beautifully. Our granddaughter was looking forward to wearing it. I romantically envisioned us at the Bat Mitzvah service, each draped by a meaningful tallit.

We called my brother in Maryland and asked him to use his keys to our house and get suits and shoes and tallitot. We told him exactly where to find each item, including ties and jewelry. He called us back and said that he had found everything on our list easily, except for my husband's new tallit.

My sister-in-law was not satisfied. A few days later, she went to our house. She stood in the bedroom and thought, "If I lived here, where would I keep a tallit?" She rummaged around and, in the back of the sock drawer, she found a velvet bag with a tallit.

Triumphantly, they brought all of our items with them to Oklahoma. We were extremely grateful and thanked them profusely. We now had the right apparel for the occasion. But . . . the tallit was not the beautiful, brand-new anniversary one. It was a small, old, worn tallit that my husband had been given by his deceased parents. He decided to wear it anyway.

The Bat Mitzvah service was inspiring. In that synagogue, the parents and grandparents have the honor of sitting on the bimah. We were up close to watch our gracious, gorgeous granddaughter lead the service, chant Torah and Haftarah in proper trope, deliver a thoughtful Dvar Torah and conduct herself with maturity and dignity. With silent satisfaction, I noted how elegantly she wore the tallit that I had lovingly made. We were so proud of her. We also felt exalted by the idea that another link in the chain of our Jewish generations had been forged.

After the service, while my husband was folding his tallit, he looked pensive. He said to my sister-in-law in a low voice, "I have not worn this tallit in a very long time. I'm glad you found this one instead of the new one. It made me feel as if my parents were here and embracing me."

Weeks later, when we were back in our own home, I searched for the missing tallit several times, but did not find it. Finally, when my back was in good enough condition, I took everything out of the likely cabinet, piece by piece. Sandwiched between two large bags I found the new velvet case enclosing the beautiful, brand-new tallit.

Unbidden tears sprang to my eyes as I tried to make sense of it all. What phenomenon was at work here? What made it so that our granddaughter was adorned in a tallit designed by her grandmother (me), I was caressed by a tallit made by my mother, and my husband felt embraced by a tallit from his parents? Was all this mere chance?

**Helen Ray Gelman Rib** is a retired Jewish educator living in Potomac, Maryland. Her four children and eight grandchildren live all across the continent from California to Massachusetts. She keeps quite busy, and especially enjoys reading Torah at her Conservative synagogue in Bethesda, Maryland. She and her husband, a retired nuclear safety engineer, spend a lot of time visiting their loved ones around the country.

# Sheltered Under a Tallit

*Dorothy Talmadge*

In October of 1976, I married my second husband, Al Talmadge, under a chuppah he created using his own tallit attached to four bamboo poles. His tallit was made of white silk with traditional blue striping. Each pole was about four feet long and was held by a man very special to each of us. One was supported by my father, Harry Bilawsky; one by my brother, Bernard Bilawsky; one by my husband's son, Wayne Talmadge; and one by my son, Roger Silverblatt, then twelve years old. This wedding, this Impossible Dream that became a reality, was held in the living room of my home in the presence of thirty people nearest and dearest to us.

The pleasure of being married at home, under this special canopy and surrounded by so much love, just radiated through the group. My daughter Pam Silverblatt, then sixteen, said she wanted the same kind of wedding when her time came. And so she did. She married her husband, Howard Tanz, in exactly the same spot, with Rabbi Sanford Jarashow officiating, the same rabbi who had married my husband and me.

My son Roger, who had been one of the chuppah holders at my wedding, was very taken by the concept of the chuppah at my wedding. When he married his sweetheart, Delilah Rugg, on June 27, 2004, he also designed his own chuppah. This time a tallit belonging to the bride's late grandfather, Martin Rugg, was used. This tallit has stripes of many colors—black, red, orange, gold, blue, and lavender—and was attached to eight-foot bamboo poles by white wooden finials.

Since the wedding ceremony was held on the outdoor deck of the bride's parents' vacation home in Kerhonkson, New York, the chuppah was carried outside by the four men who supported it. The four chuppah holders were the bride's brother, Isaac Rugg; the bride's uncle, David Goodman; the groom's brother-in-law, Howard Tanz; and the groom's cousin, Daniel Bilawsky, the son of one of my chuppah bearers. The officiating rabbi, Tsurah August of Woodstock, New York, preceded this group.

Being married under this tallit had special meaning to Roger and Delilah. Not only was it one of her grandfather's tallitot, but her grandfather had passed away just six months earlier. He had been looking forward to this marriage and had blessed it while he was alive. Under the circumstances, the bride and groom felt that her grandfather, Martin Rugg, a past president of the synagogue in Ellenville, New York, was part of the ceremony and was blessing them all over again.

In addition to using a tallit as the chuppah, the groom requested that the rabbi wrap him and his bride in the tallit that the groom had worn at his Bar Mitzvah. They were wrapped in this tallit for the saying of the seven blessings.

During the ceremony, the groom's grandmother, Helen Bilawsky, was invited to say a few words about this Bar Mitzvah tallit. She told all gathered for this happy occasion that she had been in Israel in 1967, just after the Six-Day War. At that time, the groom was just three years old. She bought the white silk tallit with blue stripes (54 x 24 inches) in Jerusalem, and brought it back to New York to be put away and saved for his Bar Mitzvah. It was used for that purpose on June 4, 1977.

Then the bride's grandmother, Clara Rugg, was invited to speak about the kiddush cup from which the joyous couple shared their sips of wine. The silver kiddush cup had been brought to this country from Russia by the bride's maternal great-great-grandfather.

Roger and Delilah had great feelings of joy and sentimentality about this wedding ceremony. They chose to be married in the personal surroundings of a family home. Being married beneath her grandfather's tallit, being wrapped in his Bar Mitzvah tallit, sipping from a silver kiddush cup that goes back four generations—all gave them a feeling of continuity, a feeling that their marriage fit seamlessly within their heritage and their ancestry.

This sense that Judaism was being passed down from generation to generation was also exemplified by the two young ring bearers, Elijah Horne and Michael Harris Tanz. Between their ages of three years old and the ages of their great-grandmothers (ninety), there is a span of eighty-seven years.

The happiness and pleasure that suffused the entire wedding is very difficult to put into words—but it is a feeling that no one who was part of this event will ever forget.

**Dorothy Bilawsky (Silverblatt) Talmadge** lives in Massapequa, New York. She is a former social worker and a retired elementary school teacher. She has two children and one grandchild.

# The Past Generation Is Forever Present

*Marden David Paru*

Mom and Dad passed away a few years ago, but they still manage to join us at celebratory occasions via a special tallit that Dad bought in Israel on an anniversary trip many years ago. They arrive, are well greeted, and are ever present, at special family events that have taken place since their demise. To date, my son, two nieces, and my brother have all been host to their dear departed relatives at memorable family occasions.

Dad, a very traditional Jew, born and ordained in Lithuania, always had a separate tallit for use on the High Holy Days. Though trained as a rabbi, he served for many years as a *hazzan* (cantor) and chanted the traditional *machzor* (daily prayer) liturgy of our people in congregations in Phoenix, Arizona, and Tulsa, Oklahoma. (As youngsters, my brother and I sang in a family choir and accompanied Dad on the pulpit.) Mom always saw to it that his High Holy Day tallit was neatly pressed and bright white, reflective of the spiritual cleansing of the soul that we go through in our atonement on Yom Kippur.

Bringing Mom and Dad to these *smichot* (life-cycle celebrations) through Dad's tallit has become a tradition that makes our family quite proud. Dad's tallit is interwoven into the fabric of these celebrations in a profound way: His tallit serves as the chuppah, the wedding canopy used in the ceremony of kiddushin.

The first wedding in which this tallit covered the bride and groom in blessings was my son's, which took place in B'nai Tikvah Congregation, a Conservative temple in North Brunswick, New Jersey. A niece was married two years later inside Congregation Agudath Sholom, an Orthodox synagogue in Stamford, Connecticut. The third chuppah, for another niece, was erected nine months later under the blue skies outside in the parking lot of a Baltimore shul to accommodate a Gerer Hassidic crowd. The tallit emerged a fourth time to celebrate the third marriage of my brother, Sheldon Paru, in the summer of 2004 on the beach at Hilton Head, South Carolina, in the presence of a small gathering of the immediate family.

In this way Mom and Dad were present at all four weddings. Their spirit could be felt flowing through Dad's tallit.

Parents are entitled to the *z'chut* (the privilege) of marrying off their children and being present at the weddings of their grandchildren. Yet that may not always be physically possible. My *abba* and *ima*, our *bubbie* and *zaydie*, have joined us at each simcha described above and, G-d willing, it will happen again soon with our daughter. This same tallit, I am confident, will also find its way into the wedding ceremonies of future generations of our family, reaffirming the heritage and presence of my beloved parents.

**Marden David Paru** and his wife Joan Kemeny, who live in Sarasota, Florida, are the parents of two adult children, Victor and Elana. Mr. Paru has held executive positions at a number of Jewish communal organizations, including the Jewish Federation of Rockland County, and Jewish federations in Montreal, Cincinnati, Passaic/Clifton (NJ), and Poughkeepsie and Kingston (NY). He currently belongs to the Association of Jewish Community Organization Personnel, the National Association of Social Workers, and he serves on the Board of the Southwest Florida Chapter of the Association of Fundraising Professionals.

# The Faces of My Family

*Ruth Israely*

I did not realize at the time how important the fiftieth anniversary of my father's Bar Mitzvah was for him. Like the simple child at Passover, I did not know to ask. My habit is to joke with people, so I gave my father a kiss, $18, and a certificate for the tree my siblings and I had planted for him in Israel. We wrote a card that said something like, "Finally, you're a man!"

At the ceremony, as he stood up for his aliyah, he looked just as terrified as he must have fifty years earlier, but he sang beautifully, wearing his beloved tallit. The tallit had not come with his parents from the snowdrifts of Latvia. It did not survive any wars in Europe or the days when my grandfather sold rags in Brooklyn. It's new and although it looks traditional enough—white with black stripes—six generations of immigrants and their descendents peer out from between the stripes at our most terrifying and joyful ceremonies.

The idea of celebrating a Bar Mitzvah anniversary came to my father from his own grandfather, who had commemorated his Bar Mitzvah at eighty-three—thirteen years after the seventy-year natural life span of a man, as designated by the Torah. My father wanted to continue this tradition. In talking with his friend Ellen Gang, an artist, my father expressed a desire for a tallit that would allow him to wrap himself in his family and that could be passed through the next generations of the family to be used at milestone ceremonies. His first tallit had appeared on the bimah at each of his children's B'nai and B'not Mitzvah. I remember threading my fingers nervously through the fringes as I read the Haftarah. At my sister's wedding, the same tallit served as a chuppah, and swaddled her first-born daughter at the baby-naming ceremony.

With the help of Ellen and my mother, my father dug through a mountain of pictures and chose twenty-three that highlighted the essence of the kind of ceremony he wanted the tallit to be used for. The large family portraits from the 1950s are the most astonishing. Taken at B'nai and B'not Mitzvah and weddings, they show the generation from the Old Country dressed in their best alongside their children and grandchildren. They wear serious expressions, reminding us that ceremonies are about both joy and responsibility.

Ellen describes my father as having been very driven to select pictures that would show the history of his family. This was an extensive project. The structure of my family is as nontraditional as the tallit itself. From my convert mother to my half-siblings to my step-aunt, to "Uncle Pickle," a guy who isn't even related to us by marriage, we are the blended family to end all blended families. Looking through the pictures became a cathartic process. It took many weeks, and, realizing that there would only be more pictures to come in the future, my father made the decision to leave space for more to be added as our family grew.

Although the pictures on the tallit don't tell a specific story, they prevent me from getting lost in a Jewish historical stereotype. When told briefly, my family's history is similar to that of so many other Jewish families: Driven from Eastern Europe to the New World in the early twentieth century, my father's family lived in relative poverty, scratching out a living through unskilled labor. After his father died at a young age, my father put himself through college and medical school. It's a Jewish-American dream, and it's just the way the history books tell the story. It gives me a sense of community, but not a sense of my own identity.

My father's tallit is the beginning of my understanding of his side of the family. When I ask my father about the pictures, I hear stories I never knew to ask about: stories about courageous people, stories about people who became embittered by a life of struggle, stories about people who didn't give up, and stories about people who did. *Tradition* is often shorthand for all the things that have come before. My father's tallit is an abbreviation, but it goes beyond culture and religion: Woven into this garment that has been worn by Jews since we wandered in the desert are the faces that stand for a set of disappointments and triumphs belonging only to my family.

**Ruth Israely** is an aspiring teacher and writer living in Chapel Hill, North Carolina.

# A Family Heirloom

### Shirley Lockshin

My parents, Ida and Joseph Goldenfeld, came to the United States on September 1, 1920, from Roumania, part of the massive wave of Jewish immigration in the early years of the twentieth century. When they were married in the Old Country on November 26, 1919, my father was twenty-three and my mother was nineteen. As a wedding present, my mother had a tallit hand-woven for my father. She made a case made out of velvet and embroidered his initial *J* on the velvet case for the tallit.

They were married under this tallit and brought it to the United States with them, where he opened a men's clothing store in Massillon, Ohio. My mother was the in-store tailor. They worked very hard together and were very well respected in the community. Besides being a great homemaker, my mother was very artistic and could make anything.

They kept the hand-woven tallit, but my father never used it because it was huge. He was a very religious man, but he used a smaller tallit for all the minyans and services and holidays. When our eldest daughter Barbara was getting married, we couldn't decide what to use as a chuppah. At one point during the wedding planning, my father said, "I have a tallit they could use. We were married under this tallit and it would be the start of a tradition in our family." Until that point, I never even knew my father had this tallit or its well-traveled history.

My parents, of blessed memory, passed away in the

mid-1990s after being married for seventy-five years. My father lived to be one hundred and my mother over ninety-five years old.

But their legacy lives on. Our two granddaughters, Barbara's children Sara and Rachel, were wrapped in this tallit for their B'not Mitzvah; and our son David's son, Sam, had this tallit draped on his shoulders for his Bar Mitzvah on Purim.

When I presented the tallit to Sam, I told him that we pray that this tradition and the meaning of this tallit will continue to inspire him throughout his life, just as I hope that it will for his brother and two sisters. I told him to learn the tradition, live the tradition, and pass it on to the next generation.

In the summer of 2005, our son's daughter will celebrate her Bat Mitzvah, and this tradition of my father's tallit will continue.

How proud my parents would be to know that their great-granddaughters and great-grandsons wore this special tallit! And all their descendents take special pride in incorporating this tallit into their *smichot* (happy occasions). To think that my mother started this tradition many, many years ago, when she had a wedding present handmade for her bridegroom in Roumania, and my father thought to tie his own wedding to his granddaughter's through an Old Country tallit that now shelters generations in the New World.

**Shirley Lockshin** and her husband Jim Lockshin, live in Canton, Ohio. They have three children and eight grandchildren.

# Jerry

*Harriet R. Goren*

O n Sundays we'd pile into the '67 Chevy and head to one of my uncles' interchangeable apartments—musty furniture, plastic slipcovers, tassled lamps. I was the only niece, and all my aunts and uncles were much older. Everyone complained about sciatica and arthritis, and I had no one to talk to except my cousin Jerry, who was sweet but said little. When I was nine, he had just come back from a year of fighting in Vietnam. He'd sit on the other side of the room in a heavy chair and smile shyly; sometimes we'd play gin rummy. I imagined that his silence accompanied wise thoughts, as he absorbed without complaint all the shrill laughter and babka-filled kisses that swirled around us. There were always whispers, rumblings: Jerry was Not Right. "It's the war," said my mother. "Who the hell knows what went on over there?"

One Sunday we were late. My father paced in front of our apartment door as I was getting zipped and swathed into layers of clothing, as if Brooklyn were the North Pole.

The telephone rang. My mother ran over and picked up the phone, and after a moment I saw her body seem to get smaller, her eyes wider. "What do you mean?" she yelled into the phone. "How could someone just disappear?" She leaned into the doorway, and I thought she might fall over.

"Are we going or not?" my father demanded.

"Jerry's missing," she answered, in almost a whisper.

MY MOTHER AND Jerry's father tried to find him, keeping a few private investigators gainfully employed. They determined that he was somewhere in San Francisco; beyond that, no clue.

Thirty years passed, and I paid the price of having old relatives: My aunts and uncles died, and then my parents. Jerry's few belongings, including a small, blue velvet bag emblazoned with a frayed, gold Star of David, ended up in a corner of my bottom drawer. Inside were the accoutrements of male Jewish adulthood: a prayer book and a tallit—a prayer shawl, pure silk embroidered white on white. Except for the image in my mind of soft eyes and dark hair when everyone else's was gray, nothing else remained of my cousin.

ONE HOT AUGUST afternoon, I checked my answering machine. "Hello?" said an unfamiliar, twangy voice. "This is the Family Research Bureau in Utah, regarding your cousin, Jerome. Please call back at your earliest convenience." He left a phone number. Then a dial tone.

I stared at the phone. Shaking, I dialed. Jerry, it seemed, had died a year ago in San Francisco, leaving a small amount of money. His veteran's benefits—which had ended up at a company that specialized in tracking down relatives of lonely people who were outlived by their bank balances—had found their way to me.

I looked out the window at the crowds going to lunch and was sad, which startled me. Jerry had long ago faded to a wisp of a thought in my awareness, the tallit bag hidden and buried beneath winter sweaters. Most of my family, these days, existed only as images with bent corners in photo albums. There, or among the anonymous people walking down the street, I had always imagined Jerry would remain.

IT WAS A month later, the second day of Rosh Hashanah. For most of my adult life I had been Jewish in name only, not caring much for a God who left me with hundreds of dollars a year in burial plot maintenance bills. But at the urging of a friend who thought it would be a good way to meet guys, I'd recently joined a synagogue, one rich in music, joy, and community. At first I was wary; I had forgotten how to be part of something larger than myself. Gradually I came to love it, and trust in its permanence, and I watched my life grow less tentative and more intertwined with others as a result. As I walked to holiday services that morning, I thought of my first connections, my family, and the stories from so long ago, and remembered the questions I still had about Jerry. What day did he die? I wondered. I had never asked.

But a few days later, before I could call Utah for the answer, I received an envelope of legal documents. Jerry had been homeless, I read. According to a court report, "He has not likely bathed in years. The social worker stated: 'He is bright (although very irrational) and has social graces. We have not included details about the condition in which his body was found, as it is very graphic.'" My tears stained the photocopies as I recognized the kind, lost boy from the back of my mind. He had died in his room the previous September, on the second day of Rosh Hashanah—the same day, exactly one year later, that I would wonder when to say kaddish for Jerry and remember his life in prayer along with the rest of our family.

It took me one more year, until the second day of the next Rosh Hashanah, to take Jerry's tallit from the small velvet bag and wrap it around myself for the first time, and so join with my community in yet another way. It was an unfamiliar sensation, a nice one, and reminded me how he would gingerly hug me good-bye, the embrace of a feather blown about however the world decreed. The Jewish tradition is to be buried in one's tallit but now, instead, I would rest his memory on my shoulders every time I wore it. And the others, my aunts and uncles, my mother and father, like the fringes bundled together and tied tightly at its corners, would never be far away.

**Harriet R. Goren** is a graphic designer who lives and works in Manhattan, where she also sings in a chamber choir and with her synagogue, Congregation B'nai Jeshurun.

# IN THE BEGINNING: THE FIRST TIME

Simple or elaborate, a tallit is suffused with spiritual overtones and under-tones from the moment a person first dons it. Traditionally, a boy was presented with his first tallit at his Bar Mitzvah. In some sects of Judaism, such as the Lubavitch Hasidim, a man does not wear a tallit until he gets married.

Over the past twenty years or so, with the parallel trends toward feminism in the larger culture and egalitarianism in Jewish practice, more and more women have been assuming obligations, or mitzvot, formerly the sole province of men—reading from the Torah, wearing a kippah, and donning a tallit.

While Orthodox practice still limits tallit-wearing to men, Conservative and Reform synagogues have increasingly encouraged young people of both sexes to perform the mitzvah of the tallit at the time of Bar or Bat Mitzvah. And the ease with which young women have adopted and embraced the practice of tallit-wearing has inspired their mothers and grandmothers to consider join-ing the ranks of tallit-wearers as well.

In most cases, the decision to assume the obligation of wearing a tallit—even for female rabbis—is not taken lightly. The essays that follow delve into what it means for people to drape themselves in a prayer shawl whose resonances go back millennia in Jewish history. Interestingly, many of the writers are older women who became b'not mitzvah as middle-aged adults. For them, the tallit represents much more than a practice now acceptable for both men and women; when the tallit falls on their shoulders for the first time, they experience a deeply felt sense of being swathed in G-d's love, being closer to G-d than ever before.

And there is no turning back. None of these women "of a certain age" find the mitzvah or obligation burdensome. Instead, they discover a spiritual depth they never knew was theirs in the warmly comforting folds of a tallit.

—Diana Drew

# A Momentous Decision

*Aileen Grossberg*

On April 19, I turned sixty. On May 4, my father died, and on May 6 I first wore a tallit. How did that come to be?

When I was a little girl, I would sit between my father and my grandfathers and twist the tzitzit on each one's tallit as he davened. Sometimes one grandfather or another would put the tallit over my shoulders and enfold me in its and his embrace. How close I felt to my father and grandfathers and to God at those moments.

As I got older, I lost interest in sitting quietly with my father and grandfathers in synagogue. I preferred to hang out with my friends, but when I did join my family in Row F, seats 10 through 16, I would still twirl those fringes and feel oh so connected.

I grew up and married a man whose relationship with tzitzit was limited to his aufruf. I never realized how much I missed that experience of sitting next to someone in shul, taking the tzitzit in my hand, and twirling and twisting and almost caressing them.

Then my daughters were born, attended religious school, and became b'not mitzvah. While my family was growing up, a revolution, albeit a quiet one, was taking place. My daughters thought nothing of reading from the Torah, taking their place beside the boys in their religious school class. However, despite my own star status in religious school—first as a student, then as a teacher—the first time I ever performed a ritual on the bimah was on my wedding day, and the next time was more than five years later when my first child was named.

Things were changing—in Judaism and in the larger world. When my older daughter became a bat mitzvah, she had an aliyah, davened a bit, and let the rabbi carry the day. A few years later, when it was my younger daughter's turn, she had an aliyah, read her maftir, and davened the Torah service wearing a tallit and a kippah. How I enjoyed the experience of shopping with her for that tallit! But for my aliyah as the mother of the bat mitzvah, my head was bare and the only garment on my shoulders was my jacket.

Every time I went to a Jewish conference or stepped into a Judaica shop, I gently caressed the tallitot, feeling the scratchiness of the wool or the slippery softness of the silk, admiring the woven colors in the stripes or the brightness of the paint on the silk.

Some of my friends began to appear in shul wrapped or draped in tallitot. I admired the ease with which they wore this ritual garment, but it didn't seem right for me to join them. Still, I had begun to wear a kippah whenever I entered the sanctuary of my synagogue, which required women on the bimah to cover their heads but made no such regulation for those sitting in the congregation.

A few years ago, I decided to mark Rosh Hodesh with my Sunday School class of first- and second-graders. Looking for a way to signal that something special was going to happen, I brought my daughter's tallit to school, dramatically kissed the atarah, and placed the tallit gingerly across my shoulders. The moment was magical for me, and the children sensed that, too. That magical feeling returned every month as I repeated the ceremony and the words heralding the next Jewish month.

At about the same time, I decided that when I turned sixty in a few years, I would get my own tallit. Perhaps I saw that landmark birthday as so far away that I had lots of time to make the decision; perhaps I saw it as a way to mark another phase of life: the children out of the house, one married; my mother gone and my elderly father not much concerned about or aware of the life changes in his children.

Last fall I went to an Israeli fair and saw beautiful tallitot. I felt the wool and stroked the silk. I admired the vibrant stripes and the bright silk paints, and, attracted by the shimmering colors, I bought a tallit months before that landmark birthday.

Almost every day I tried it on. Did it hang too low? Did it sit on my shoulders correctly? How should I gather the tzitzit? Do I tent myself in the tallit when I first put it on? It all looks so natural when I watch the men and even the boys in the congregation. Did they, too, have these questions or is tallit-wearing an instinctive behavior among male Jews?

My birthday was just days away. Would I or wouldn't I? I was beseiged by questions: My tallit—is it too boldly colored? Is it a fashion statement rather than a statement of religious commitment? Will everyone stare at me? Will I trip, rip, catch the tzitzit? Will my grandchildren sit beside me in shul and twist and braid the tzitzit? Will I drape my tallit over their shoulders as my father and grandfathers did to me? Will they remember and do the same for their grandchildren?

I PUT THE tallit in its colorful bag on the front seat of the car. I took it with me to the synagogue, but it never went into the building.

Then came the call. My father had died. I put things in order at home and my husband and I drove up to Boston, heavy-hearted. I was now an orphan. I would never sit beside my father again. I packed my tallit along with my funeral suit, the slippers for the shiva at my brother's house, since there was no longer a family home, and an appropriate book to read, for, like my father, I must always have a book by my side. I brought Ari Friedman's *A Year of Kaddish*.

The funeral was over and we went to my brother's synagogue for *Shacharit* the next morning. I brought my tallit along. But this time I brought it not just to the building but into the building. I unzipped the bag and took out the colorful prayer shawl. I said the bracha—

how did I know the words?—kissed the atarah as if by instinct, and draped the tallit around my shoulders. It fell just as it should. It felt as if I had been wearing that garment all my life. This was the right time.

It was Shabbat and my brothers and I returned to the shul where we had grown up. It was a shadow of its former glory, a beautiful building with few people to fill it. We sat in the seats where our family had sat for over seventy-five years. Now there were many women wearing tallitot. I had no one to enfold me in a tallit. Nor did I need anyone: I had brought my own. I was now taking my father's place among the people of Israel.

Each morning as I sit in minyan, I realize that I may no longer be able to sit by my father's side and twist the tzitzit, but I can carry on the tradition myself and perhaps someday my grandson or granddaughter will sit by my side and continue the chain that goes back generations, from father to father and son to daughter.

**Aileen Thrope Grossberg**, originally from Lowell, Massachusetts, lives in Montclair, New Jersey, where she is active in Congregation Shomrei Emunah. Mrs. Grossberg serves as volunteer librarian for her synagogue; she also works as a school librarian in Livingston, New Jersey, and as a reference librarian at the Montclair Public Library. She has taught primary-aged children for over twenty-five years at B'nai Shalom in West Orange, New Jersey. She is a member of CAJE and the Association of Jewish Libraries (AJL), and is active in Hadassah. Mrs. Grossberg is married and has two adult daughters.

# My Tallit Speaks . . .

### Bernice Todres

I was one of the lucky ones. I was sent to Celebrations, the store of the Jewish Museum in New York City. I was laid on a glass shelf under beautiful lighting. I had not been there long when she first touched me. I started wondering that day who would choose me, and now I wondered if it would be her. She touched me somehow with such awe . . . and yet she did not take me home. For a moment I felt bereft, imagining myself as a child in an orphanage waiting to be chosen, to be taken into a home and a family. For me, it was a longing to be wrapped around her.

She returned quite soon. It had been like love at first sight after all. The next day she carried me in her arms, since I did not come with a tallit bag. That was how it happened that I became so close to her. She always carried me to morning minyan and back, holding me close in her bare hands, never laying me down just anywhere. Then there was the first time I was draped around her and the first day she kissed my tzitzit, ever so gently. What a journey we are making together, I thought. I felt so blessed to be hers.

It was her year of saying kaddish for her mother, and so I know I was more than her prayer shawl. I was her comfort on days I could feel her entire frame sobbing beneath me, and also on days when her tears flowed quietly.

One day, quite unexpectedly, she lifted me from her shoulders to cover her head during the *Amidah*. Not all tallitot have a chance to do this, so I was not sure how it would feel or what it would mean. These times when I have covered her head have become the holiest moments in both our lives. At these times I know that she longs for *devekut* (spiritual oneness with God), and to be able to protect her in this way is indeed holy.

So what a shock it was after only two years—especially the year of saying kaddish—to hear her tell Morty, her friend, that she was getting a new tallit. We cried together that last morning minyan as we prayed together. I did not allow myself to ask "Why?" I know this is life. Our journey together lasted only two years, yet it was intense, as we prayed together every morning and were especially close for almost three hours every Shabbat.

One other thing I will always remember. It happened during a class she attended on Jewish burial. There I heard her decide to be buried with me wrapped around her. I could hardly catch my breath knowing that. Although it is a time far off, God willing, I long for that moment of being wrapped around her once again and forever.

Some people are always there, always part of our life. Others we know only briefly, yet without words we feel deeply connected to them all the days of our lives. Such memories live forever in our hearts and souls.

**Bernice Todres** lives on the Upper West Side in Manhattan. A teacher of meditation, she is on the faculty of Makom, The Center for Mindfulness, at the JCC on the Upper West Side. She is also a lecturer and workshop leader both in the United States and Europe, with a private practice in Mindfulness-based Stress Reduction on Madison Avenue. She is the mother of Rachelle, Nadia, and Jonathan Todres.

# My Tallit Enfolds Me

## *Sheila Rubin*

I was raised in a classical Reform temple where no one would think to wear a tallit or a kippah. There, the atmosphere was cool and the decorum proper. As a wife and mother, I wanted to join a Reform congregation that offered warmth and spirituality and the freedom to embrace the ritual of the tallit and the custom of wearing the kippah.

My children wore tallitot on the occasion of their B'nai Mitzvah. Our daughter, however, elected not to wear hers again. It lay wrapped in tissue paper in the bottom of my cedar chest along with other things too precious to discard. As time passed, tallitot began to appear on the shoulders of some of the women in my congregation. I didn't feel comfortable enough to try it there. I did not want to be caught up in a "fad."

Then my husband and I went on an adult kallah weekend. We had attended this weekend several times in the past, and I looked forward to the love and peacefulness I always felt there. Kallah was held at Camp Harlam, the Reform Jewish camp in the Pocono Mountains of Pennsylvania. The outdoor synagogue on the hill, the relaxed and casual surroundings, the participation of everyone in the worship experience enticed me to approach each new religious encounter with curiosity and awe.

Perhaps this is why I packed my daughter's tallit along with my sweats and sneakers. Her father, of blessed memory, and I had selected it for her so many years ago. The twelve tribes of Israel were beautifully portrayed in the colors of the rainbow. I felt comfortable at kallah, ready to try a new ritual. Although a bit uneasy, I made the decision to put the tallit on.

With the loving care of a dear friend, Barbara Stoner, and the blessing and song of then–song leader Cantor Leon Shur, I wrapped myself in the folds of my daughter's rainbow tallit—the rainbow a reminder of God's covenant with humankind. It felt right! As a mother and grandmother, this has since become a wonderful ritual for me.

Now, on Yom Kippur and whenever Torah is read, I enfold myself in this multicolored tallit to pray, and find myself transported to a special place where I am embraced with spirituality and feel open to God.

**Sheila Rubin** is a member of Temple Shalom in Aberdeen, New Jersey, where she sits on the Board of Trustees. She has eight grandchildren and is married to Phil Rubin, Immediate Past President of the congregation.

# Tallit for a Late Bat Mitzvah

*Davi Walders*

A hundred generations after Tamar,
in the year of her own jubilee,
a woman still hungers for Torah.
She will be cold on the bimah
alone. Gone are the arms of family.
Only a longing for the threads
of their blessing remains.

She has never worn a tallit,
never even thought of it.
But she is older now
and will be cold on the bimah
alone. Tamar's words whisper
of necessity's sudden impulse,
a sudden turning, of choosing

a new path, mountains, gold
and green, woven with words
into pure wool to cover
shoulders, breasts, heart.
Threads of family, weft
of generations, Torah and haftarah
wisdom on a woman's tallit.

Blue tzitzit cornered
and tied. Wearing words,
chanting words, "*Vayet eleha
el haderech*. And he turned
towards her on the path."
Warmed by words and old
worlds. Holding them close.

**Davi Walders** is a poet, writer, and educator, who lives in Chevy Chase, Maryland. Her poetry and prose have been published in more than 150 anthologies and other publications, including the *American Scholar*, *Ms.*, and *JAMA*. She developed and directs the Vital Signs Poetry Project at the National Institutes for Health, and received Hadassah of Greater Washington's 2002 Myrtle Wreath Award for this work.

# To Daven Like a Man

*Mindy Sandel*

I grew up in Irvington, New Jersey, in an Orthodox Jewish household in the 1950s and '60s. My family belonged to Congregation Ahavath Achim Bikur Cholim, an Orthodox synagogue where I went to Hebrew school. The shul's name means "Loving Brothers [and Sisters] Who Visit the Sick."

I was always very interested in Judaism, and won many awards as a student in the Hebrew school. However, I would constantly get into arguments with Rabbi Leon Yagod because I thought it wasn't fair that I would never be allowed to lead a service in Hebrew simply because I was female, even though I was an excellent student and knew all the prayers.

I did not have a Bat Mitzvah. Orthodox girls did not do that. I could not go up on the bimah and read from the Torah. Boys who didn't know Hebrew well enough to pray in our holy language could lead prayers in Hebrew and stumble though Torah readings at their B'nai Mitzvah while I was never given the opportunity to even learn to read the fancy Torah script. All I could ever do was sit with the other women in the synagogue, separate from the men.

Women would constantly say to me, "You daven [pray] like a man." I heard this odd compliment not just in my own synagogue but in all synagogues where I would pray throughout my life. How can I daven like a man? I do not wear a kippah. I do not wear a tallit. All I could look forward to was someday wearing a head-covering in the synagogue once I was married—no kippah, no tallit. Despite my disappointment, I embraced Orthodox practice; I would not go against anything Orthodox.

When my younger brother, Benjamin, prepared for his Bar Mitzvah, I was the one who helped him learn the prayers. He had such a hard time learning them. When the tallit was placed on his shoulders for the first time, I looked at him with tremendous pride. Yet, no one had ever looked at me with such pride. This he always remembered.

I went to college in Israel. Living in a small town, Kiryat Tivon, near Haifa, I continued to go to synagogue every Saturday morning, and, tucked away in the back with other women, I still heard that line—"You daven like a man." Yet again the same thought came to mind. How can I daven like a man? I do not wear a kippah. I do not wear a tallit.

I married Haim in Israel, came back to New Jersey, had two children—Leah and Ron—and joined a Conservative synagogue, Temple Hatikvah, in Flanders, New Jersey, which was unlike any other synagogue I had attended. I wore the traditional women's head-covering because I was married. Most women in the synagogue did not even wear that. But here women counted in the minyan; they could lead a service, and they could read from the Torah. A woman could wear a kippah and a tallit if she chose to. Yet I didn't. I couldn't. It was too strange. It went against everything I knew to be Jewish. I would participate in services, sitting together with men wearing kippot and tallitot, but I would not put either of these on.

On February 28, 1990, I was involved in a nearly fatal automobile accident. I was in a coma. I was on a respirator. I had to have a tracheotomy. I had a feeding tube. I had to undergo hemodialysis. My liver was lacerated. Many bones were broken. My face was all but destroyed. According to medical statistics, I was not supposed to survive. Yet I did! In August 1990 I returned home from the hospital in a wheelchair.

I endured years of therapy. I had to relearn to walk, to talk, to function. In all, I underwent ten years of surgeries, large and small. My last "major" surgery took place in October 1991—an operation that required numerous surgeons all working together (three or four oral-facial-cranial surgeons, an orthopedic surgeon, an ophthalmologist, a neurosurgeon, a plastic surgeon); sixteen hours of surgery; and a two-week hospital stay. My face was rebuilt. My jaws were rebuilt and had to be wired shut to heal. When I woke up in intensive care, I could not talk. I said a prayer of thanks that I was still alive and then I said to myself, I want to have a Bat Mitzvah to thank G-d that I am alive. I want to lead a service. I want to learn how to read the Torah. I want to wear a tallit.

Six weeks after I returned home and the wires were removed from my mouth, I phoned Rabbi Herman Cohen and told him that I wanted to have a Bat Mitzvah. The date was to be Saturday, April 4, 1992.

The Sunday before, March 29, my brother Benjamin and I went to the cemetery in Fairview, New Jersey, to visit the graves of our parents before the Bat Mitzvah. On the way home we passed a Judaica store that happened to be going out of business. I suggested we stop in. If the Bat Mitzvah had been scheduled for a later date, the store would have been closed for good. My brother bought me a pink tallit to wear for my Bat Mitzvah, together with a pink tallit bag to protect it. He remembered all the times I had wanted to get up and lead the service as a child.

On April 4 my pink tallit was put on my shoulders in front of the synagogue. I was so proud. Sadly, my father wasn't there to share this moment, to feel the pride he had felt so many years ago when he put the tallit on my brother's shoulders. But would he have felt that same pride, since I was a daughter, not a son, I wondered. I believe he would have been just as proud of me becoming a bat mitzvah as he had been when my brother became a bar mitzvah.

I stood on the bimah in front of my family and all my friends in the congregation and led the entire service, chanted the entire Torah portion and Haftarah, wearing my pink tallit. As I prayed, I kept grabbing the fringes.

My husband, Haim, beamed with pride at my accomplishment. That is what I had always wanted—to wear a tallit with pride, my own pride and others' as well. Finally, my lifelong dream became a reality.

**Mindy Sandel**, a Jewish educator who now lives in Phoenix, Arizona, still wears her pink tallit to services regularly at Congregation Har Zion in Scottsdale, a Conservative synagogue, where she teaches in the Hebrew school. Occasionally, she leads parts of the service and chants from the Torah.

# With Strings Attached

## By Felice Sachs

Wearing a tallit was never on my radar screen until well after my Bat Mitzvah. And, I didn't become a bat mitzvah until I was forty-one years old. Like all the clothes I had to grow into as a child because my mother bought them bigger than I was at the time, I had to grow into wearing a tallit, too. Unlike other garments, this was not a physical matter, but rather an emotional and philosophical accommodation.

Growing up in a Reform congregation in Chicago, the traditional custom of men wearing tallitot for prayer was not a commonplace sight. Seeing men, in person or in pictures, wrapped in oversized white and black prayer shawls conjured up a sense of the exotic, like the painting by Marc Chagall, titled *The Praying Jew* (1923).

Jumping many years ahead, now as a wife and the mother of two boys, our family was settling into congregational life at a Conservative synagogue in Louisville, Kentucky. In this milieu, a man wearing a tallit in prayer was a given. But women wearing tallitot was not at all common.

The first time I ever saw a woman wearing a tallit is imprinted on my mind. It was a quiet Shabbat morning, still early in the service in congregational time, and it must have been in the summer. I remember the feeling of cool air pouring out of the sanctuary as I entered it. I saw the figure of a tall, lone women on the other side of the sanctuary wrapped in a generously sized, traditionally male, white and black tallit. That sight was somehow thrilling to me. I was viscerally impressed. Yet it would be several years before I felt ready to take on the responsibility of wearing a tallit myself.

I began taking adult education classes at our synagogue as our older son was beginning afternoon Hebrew school in third grade. I felt the need to become more knowledgeable about Judaism and the Hebrew language. I loved the classes with our rabbi and cantor. As the Hebrew class whittled down to a small group of women preparing for individual Bat Mitzvah, I was swept up, somewhat hesitantly, in that direction, too. Over the succeeding years the *parashat Haazinu*, which I prepared for my Bat Mitzvah, has become a "signature" reading. A friend and I have chanted that Torah portion and its Haftarah for so many years that we are known as the "*Haazinu* tag team."

After several more years of growing involvement with our synagogue, which included a stint as Sunday School principal, I was about to become the first female president of the congregation. I felt ready to embrace the commitment of wearing a tallit. Creating my own ritual garment was important to me.

Although the tallit is a simple fringed rectangle of fabric, there are rules that set it apart from any other shawl. Finding the right piece of cloth turned into one adventure. Learning the laws of *shatnez* (the biblical prohibition against mixing linen and wool) and acquiring appropriate tzitzit were other adventures in the process. It was during the assembling of the tallit that the garment began to speak to me.

My mind kept hearing the phrase "with strings attached." As I sewed, I thought about how popular culture in the late 1980s valued the freedom and casualness of situations that boasted of "no strings attached." Judaism took the opposite view, I thought. Jewish religious practice definitely had "strings attached." As an ancient yet sophisticated legal system, Judaism reaches into virtually every aspect of life. The tallit exemplifies that broad reach. The tzitzit, the "strings attached," are the reminders of a legal system that tells us it does matter how we conduct our lives and our relationships.

Since creating my tallit about sixteen years ago, I

have helped other people create tallitot of their own. Sometimes I simply talk about what is required of a tallit or go with someone to the fabric store to "try on" materials and choose one that will become her tallit. Occasionally, I demonstrate the macramé-like knotting procedure proscribed to tie the tzitzit. I have shared some of my enthusiasm and experience by co-teaching classes on tallit making. Numerous times I have had the opportunity to help someone create a tallit from its inception, choosing the fabric and embellishments, sewing the garment, and then participating in the tying of the tzitzit. I always enjoy whatever part I play in the process.

Wearing my tallit continues to be stimulating. There is the actual warmth and physicality of being wrapped in it. The rituals associated with the tzitzit heighten my consciousness of the garment's purpose. At the point in the service when the four tzitzit are gathered for the *Shema*, I look at them and think of their symbolism. The 613 mitzvot and the ingathering of the four corners of the world are two associations that come to mind when I hold the tzitzit. This simple garment with ancient roots invokes very contemporary concerns. The "strings attached" focus the tallit-wearer on the possibility of peace and unity in a world that seems to be unraveling.

**Felice Sachs** lives in Louisville, Kentucky, with her husband Bob Sachs. They are affililated with Congregation Adath Jeshurun in Louisville. A registered nurse by profession, Mrs. Sachs recently completed a master's degree in art and is currently chair of the Louisville Area Fiber and Textile Artists organization.

# Singing in Her Heart

## Dolly Grobstein

I was sixty-six years old when I finally bought myself a tallit. I was raised in a classical Reform congregation at a time when the Bat Mitzvah had not yet been introduced. And so I watched as first my older brother and then the boys in my religious school classes each celebrated becoming a bar mitzvah, which allowed them to wear a tallit and recite the blessings over the Torah.

I longed to participate in those rituals, but it was simply not done in those days. Years later, I did get the opportunity to recite the Torah blessings and I did so, but I still did not put on a tallit. When my three daughters each became a bat mitzvah, the wearing of a tallit by a woman was rare and was not included in their ceremonies either.

As years passed, I noticed that many of the younger women in our congregation had begun to wear tallitot. Still, perhaps out of shyness, I did not buy one for myself.

In February of 2000, my husband and I joined a group in our synagogue on a trip to Israel, our first. While there, I attended a Bar Mitzvah at one of Israel's few Reform congregations. The rabbi was a woman, wearing a tallit, of course. The *gabbai* (Torah checker) was also a woman, young, possibly still a teenager, and wearing a beautiful, shocking pink, hand-painted silk tallit—a woman's tallit! My desire to wear a tallit, which had been suppressed for years, suddenly surfaced and was intense.

Still, when I returned home I did nothing. Later that year my rabbi, Joel Soffin, purchased a tallit made by Ethiopian Jews. Woven of soft wool, it was done in the Joseph style, with brightly colored stripes, including some with checker work, which is mentioned in Exodus in the description of the high priest's garments. The weaving was not as refined as the commercially made ones; the soft wool has slubs that one dare not cut. But the tallit was beautiful and I loved it. I got the number of the agency importing these tallitot and called it. Unfortunately, at that time the agency had neither a catalog nor a Web site, so there was no way to view the various styles. And since my rabbi's tallit was also enormous, far larger that I would be able to handle, I was stymied.

Finally, about a year later, I decided to forge ahead and get some kind of tallit. By then I had decided against silk and had given up hope of finding an Ethiopian-made one. I went to my synagogue's Judaica shop and tried several on, but wasn't really happy. Then I learned that Rabbi Soffin had purchased several other Ethiopian tallitot, all of them smaller than his own, and that he was happy to make them available.

There were three of them: one with traditional blue and white striping, one with traditional black and white striping, and one with bright, crayola-colored stripes of red, yellow, blue, black and green. And that is the one I bought!

It took wearing it to two services for me to finally feel comfortable wearing a tallit. I felt very awkward the first time, a little less so the second. But by the third time, the tallit was truly mine. And I discovered that wearing it somehow draws me deeper into the service. It focuses me on the liturgy. I don't like to say that wearing a tallit makes me feel more Jewish, since I have always identified strongly with my Jewishness. Yet in some sense it does. Perhaps it is because I no longer feel as if I were on the outside looking in, which is how I had felt whenever I visited an Orthodox synagogue and how I had felt as I watched my brother and then my classmates become entitled to wear one of these prayer shawls. Perhaps it is comparable to attaining full citizenship—I had known for years that I could have it; I simply had to act.

There is an epilogue to this tale. My tallit did not come with a bag in which to transport it. Earlier this year, Rabbi Soffin led a group to Ethiopia. (I was not part of it.) He returned from the trip with beautiful embroideries, made by men at the Jewish compound in Addis Ababa. Most depicted scenes from Scripture or from Jewish life. Some were challah covers, some matzah covers, and, to my delight, some were tallit bags. So now my Ethiopian-made tallit has a home in a beautiful Ethiopian-made, hand-embroidered bag. The scene on mine shows King David with his harp; he is composing a psalm as Bathsheba and others look on. And I, who carry a tune with some uncertainty, find myself turning to a verse in Psalm 98:

> Shout unto the Eternal, all the earth;
> Break forth and sing for joy, yea, sing praises.

Each time I recite the blessing and put on my tallit, in my heart I am singing.

**Dolly Grobstein** was born in New Brunswick, New Jersey, and named, educated, confirmed, and married in Anshe Emeth Memorial Temple, a classical Reform synagogue in that city. In the early 1960s, she and her husband David settled in Randolph, New Jersey, and joined Temple Shalom, a young Reform congregation in neighboring Roxbury Township. During the early years of their membership, Mrs. Grobstein was chairman first of the Ritual Committee and subsequently of the Social Action Committee, while Mr. Grobstein served on the Board and eventually became President of the congregation. Since her retirement from editing, Mrs. Grobstein has returned to social action activities, working through the synagogue to serve at the Community Soup Kitchen. The Grobsteins have three daughters and five grandchildren.

# My Shelter of Peace

## Sondra Levin

You might say I came from a "mixed" marriage—
my mother was brought up in an Orthodox
household and my father in a Reform one.
Although I attended Sunday School at the Reform temple, I went to Hebrew School after regular school four
days a week at the Orthodox shul around the corner,
because mom didn't drive and this was more conven-
ient. Both my parents were active in the Reform temple
to which we belonged. Consequently, I felt very comfortable when the two congregations where I currently live
merged into one Conservative synagogue. My husband
and I have been active in the synagogue ever since.

The Conservative rabbi awakened in me a hunger
for more Jewish education and a desire to keep a kosher
home, as my mother had when I was growing up.
Hebrew lessons and a new interest in liturgical music
made me want to learn even more. By this time, our children were attending Jewish summer camps and coming
home with even more stimulating ideas on how to be
Jewish.

When our daughter became a cantor and Bar/Bat
Mitzvah tutor, my desire to begin a course of Jewish
study became much more intense. She helped me find a
program of Jewish studies at Spertus College in Chicago,
and I enrolled in Spertus' distance learning master's program in Jewish Studies, where I slowly completed my
degree.

During this time, Shabbat services began to mean
much more to me, mainly because of the inspirational

instructors and study materials at Spertus. After graduation, while I was searching for more learning opportunities, my husband and children presented me with a
beautiful tallit.

Its shiny gold and silver threads interwoven through
the white linen thrill me each Shabbat as I chant the
bracha and wrap the tallit around my shoulders. The tallit helps me focus on the service as it enfolds me in my
own little shelter of peace. I feel closer to God and to my
inner spirit while I am wearing it. I shall always be grateful to my family for encouraging me to spread my wings
and search for more opportunities for learning so that I
could satisfy the inner voice that constantly searches for
meaning in the things I do. The tallit is both a tangible
symbol of God's protection and of the path I have chosen in life.

**Sondra Levin** is the education director at Temple B'nai Shalom in
Benton Harbor, Michigan.

# A Hug From God

## Sandy Rosenfield

I am a Jew-by-Choice. The story of my conversion and Bat Mitzvah is the story of why I choose to wear a tallit.

I married my husband, Artie, thirty-one years ago. At that time, I was not Jewish. For a while, my husband and I chose to celebrate all of our holidays. Neither of us was particularly observant, except for these holiday events, but the Jewish holidays sparked something spiritual in me.

As is often the case, the wonderful news of a baby on the way prompts a couple to consider the direction their spirituality should take. Artie and I were no different. We began to talk about the traditions we wanted in our home and for our children. But, sadly, those talks were set aside when our daughter, Jennifer Lynn, was born prematurely. Though she was part of our lives for only a day, she had a tremendous impact on our lives. Children were to be an important part of our lives. We decided to adopt. Two wonderful sons, first Joshua Adam and then Joel Tyson, came into our lives and as a family we were complete.

With Joshua's arrival, we were back to The Discussion: Is ours a Jewish home? It was important to my husband that our children be raised in the Jewish religion. Still wrestling with my own spiritual path, I agreed, with the stipulation that my husband become more observant. And so it was that we chose Judaism.

My Jewish education began with our annual trips to Binghamton, New York, where we attended High Holy

Day services at Temple Israel with Artie's parents. I watched as my husband and father-in-law carefully took their tallitot out of their bags, said the bracha, and, with one smooth, circular motion, wrapped themselves in tradition. My father-in-law, Sam, would sit next to me and tell me about what was happening in the service. He was my own private tutor and I learned.

Joshua started religious school and I began my formal Jewish education. Helping him to learn, I learned more about the holidays, I learned to read Hebrew, and I learned that I needed to know more about Judaism. I spoke with the rabbi and said that I was interested in conversion. To learn more and to help my children with their religious education, I enrolled in Introduction to Judaism and I became committed to conversion. As my second son, Joel, put it, "Mommy is getting Jewish." And so, I chose Judaism and it chose me.

After the Beit Din and the mikvah came my conversion service. As I had chosen to wrap myself in Jewish traditions, rituals, and history, I decided that I would also choose to wrap myself in a tallit and wear a kippah. This was an important commitment for me, not only as an open declaration of my Judaism, but also as something I was doing for my daughter, Jenny. Thirteen years had passed since the day of her birth and it would have been her Bat Mitzvah. In memory of Jenny and my grandmother, Phoebe, I took the Hebrew name Penina bat Avraham v'Sarah. I carefully chose a beautiful, pale blue tallit with the twelve tribes on it in loving memory of my daughter. As I wore our tallit on the day of my conversion, I felt that I had made a connection with my daughter: It was as if she were giving me a hug each time I put it on. I wore our tallit to High Holy Day services. I took it out of its bag and, this time, I said the bracha with Artie and Grandpa Sam. As I sat in the sanctuary with my husband and sons, having that tallit around me was like having my daughter with us and our family was complete. It was healing for me. It was then that I decided to continue my Judaic studies and become a bat mitzvah.

One of the things I like best about Reform Judaism is

its commitment to social action, and at Temple Shalom, in Succasunna, New Jersey, this commitment is extraordinary. One of the more memorable projects for me was the Ukraine project. The former Soviet republic had dropped its ban on openly practicing Judaism. Demonstrating our support for our coreligionists halfway around the world, Temple Shalom adopted a group of Russian Jews in a Ukrainian town and helped them to find and practice their Judaism again. Part of this project was to help them build a place in which they could worship and to acquire ritual items, which would enable them to conduct services. One of the requests was for tallitot. They could be donated or purchased for donation, but we needed to send as many as we could.

When I heard about the rabbi's request for tallitot, I thought that this might be something meaningful for me to do as I prepared for my Bat Mitzvah. The Russian Jews we were helping were starting a new journey as their synagogue community came to life. They were writing a new chapter in their history and I had a tallit with a story. Before giving it to the rabbi, I wrote the story of my tallit in a letter and then gave it along with my tallit to the rabbi to take with him on his next trip to the Ukraine. I don't know who was wearing my tallit, but when I saw pictures of Temple Shalom, Ukraine (yes, they named their synagogue after ours), I knew that whoever received it would take good care of it.

I was now preparing for my Bat Mitzvah and the service was coming up quickly. However, I had no tallit to wear. My family suggested that we go to the Lower East Side of Manhattan. There, we could search the Judaica shops to find just the right one for me. That day, we started a new family tradition. Whenever we needed to purchase a ritual item, we would plan a shopping day together in the city. Sure, we could have ordered something through our temple Judaica shop as we have for many other items. But for our milestone Judaica we wanted to attach a story, a memory.

That day Artie, Joshua, Joel, and I went to the Lower East Side together. We looked in many different shops for my Bat Mitzvah tallit. I wanted a big one. Finally, we went into an older shop. There were many tallitot stacked on many shelves. In the back of the shop, there was a scribe repairing Torah scrolls. This had to be the store in which I would find my tallit. I described what I wanted to the Orthodox gentleman behind the counter. Patiently, he showed me tallit after tallit until I found mine. I tried it on. It was perfect. I picked out a bag to go with it. It matched the stripes on my tallit and had my Hebrew name embroidered on it. With this tallit, I would start the next leg of my Jewish journey.

My Bat Mitzvah was coming up fast. I remembered how nervous I was about asking Uncle Jake to present me with my tallit. You see, Uncle Jake, my father-in-law's brother, was the son of an Orthodox rabbi and he, along with Grandpa Sam, had been one of my Judaic tutors. Unsure of how he would feel about presenting a tallit to a woman, I cautiously asked his son if he thought his father would do this for me. Lenny simply said, "Ask him." The rest is, as they say, history. Uncle Jake wrote the following:

Dear Sandy,

You have undertaken a huge task.

I am certain that somewhere along the line you have been dissuaded and discouraged from going through with this, and this was a proper procedure.

But, you have prevailed in your wishes, which is all to your credit and determination.

I must mention that this prayer shawl, tallit, has a great meaning, significance and power, because it is ordained in Places in the Bible and in Places in our Daily Prayers. Just quoting part of the text reads: "Speak unto the children of Israel and bid them, that they make them a Fringe upon the Corners of their Garments, throughout their generations."

Sandy, this is your garment, to cherish and use in good health for many, many years together with Artie, Josh and Joel.

As I looked at my Bat Mitzvah album while writing this story, I came across something I wrote for this occasion.

Wrapped in my tallit, I feel Your presence as I sit in Your house. Today, I sit among many and celebrate my commitment to Judaism. Other times, I come to You alone, to sit here by myself. All the time, I come to be near You, for out of the silence, You've made Yourself known to me just as surely as if You had spoken out loud.

I come to You for many reasons: for guidance and comfort, to celebrate or to rest and feel the calm. As I sit with You, I ask only for Your support in my striving for righteousness.

Though the vastness of Your being is beyond my comprehension, I do know that You are essential to my existence. Help me to make wise choices and then have the courage and conviction to act on them. Let me be thankful for what You have given me. Help me to acknowledge my flaws, learn from my mistakes and become a better person for having erred. Having requested all this, let me leave Your house to use well that for which I have asked.

Sitting in the sanctuary, alone, the silence, the sound of aleph, surrounds me and God's presence is overwhelming as I remember this prayer. I take out my big tallit and say the bracha. Then with one smooth, circular motion I wrap the garment and the memories around me. I am wrapped in a hug from God.

**Sandy Rosenfield** lives with her husband Art, sons Joel and Josh, and grandson Aidan in Landing, New Jersey. She is a member of Temple Shalom in Succasunna, New Jersey, where she sings in the choir; performs with Nefashot, a contemporary Jewish music ensemble; teaches religious school; is an advisor for Junior Congregation; writes articles for the synagogue newsletter; and does publicity for the Temple Shalom Sisterhood. Ms. Rosenfield is particularly proud of the CD Nefashot produced to feed Jewish Ethiopian children (visit www.shalomethiopia.org).

# Only the Right Tallit Will Do

## Rabbi Judith Edelstein

Tallasim, as they were referred to in my childhood home, were a known entity, although they were not worn often. My beloved Aunt Fay (z"l), a long-time friend of the family who never married, was the manager of a small tallis factory on the Lower East Side. My mother (z"l) earned pennies when she was six years old tying knots in the tzitzit. That was where my ties to tallasim ended. My only memories of the males in my family wearing tallasim are limited to the 16mm home movies of my brothers' B'nai Mitzvot. In fact, my knowledge and experience was so limited that I did not realize in those days that it was inappropriate for women to wear them. What did seem strange to me, however, was the first time I went to a Reform synagogue in the 1970s and nary a tallis or yarmulke was in sight.

A quick jump from the 1950s, when my first impressions of Jewish tradition were formed, based on a few forays into my grandfather's *shtiebl* (small Hasidic synagogue), to the 1960s when things were turned upside down, including Jewish practice. *The Jewish Catalogue* was published and all things became possible within a spiritual and *haimesh* (comfortable, down-to-earth) practice.

Leap ahead to the '70s and '80s when women, after much struggle, started to become rabbis and cantors. Skip to 1992, my first year in rabbinical school. Almost all the women in my seminary wore tallitot, which made me feel compelled me to wear one as well. I did not believe I was worthy enough yet to have earned the right to wear this awesome garment, which symbolized so much commitment as well as responsibility. It was also the year of my daughter's Bat Mitzvah. I assumed that I needed one for that momentous occasion, as did she. As I obsessed over what to do, my mother handed me my deceased father's tallis. Problem solved?

No, because I was ambivalent about my father's tallis. It was one of those white, blue-striped, synthetic ones with a yellow atarah found at synagogues on a rack for people (mostly men) who failed to bring their own. More significant was that my father was not an observant Jew, so it was not as if his tallis held spiritual significance. After I learned that a man should be buried in his tallis with the tzitzit of one corner cut, my confusion increased. Nevertheless, I eventually decided to dry clean it for my daughter to wear since I was spiritually not ready.

A week before the Bat Mitzvah, I placed the tallis in my shopping cart to bring to the dry cleaners. When I arrived at the cleaners, I was dismayed. The cart was empty. I retraced my steps for ten blocks and did not find it. All of a sudden, having that particular tallis became an urgent matter. But I was never to see it again: It disappeared forever in the New York City streets. My mother was disappointed. Emotionally unable to purchase one at that point, my daughter and I appeared at her Bat Mitzvah tallisless.

Over the course of the following year, the word *obsession* took on new meaning as I searched for the "perfect" tallit (no longer thinking of it as a tallis). I believed that I would find it once I was actually prepared to own it, responsibilities and all. I scoured local Judaica stores and then searched high and low in Israel. I had fantasies about a prayer shawl that included all the colors of the rainbow. Occasionally I found a tallit that came close, but there was always something wrong with it—too expensive, too garish, or not colorful enough. I was very disappointed. If I had not been able to make my purchase in the Holy Land, would I ever find the right one?

I returned from Eretz Israel with two that were temporary, but they did not feel like me, so I did not wear them. Perhaps my spirit had not yet reached the heights required to wrap myself in the Holy One's mitzvot. That year I koshered my kitchen and began to attend *Shacharit* services most mornings as well as Shabbat services. I started leyning and wearing tefillin, too.

Then, just as I was about to give up, it appeared. I found my beloved tallit at an annual Judaica crafts fair right in my neighborhood (across the street, no less). It was like nothing I had been drawn to previously. Yet it seemed to resonate with my newly observant self at its innermost depth. Rather than the bright rainbow I had been seeking so assiduously, this one's colors were muted. Blue and red threads were intertwined between light gold panels sewn onto a cream-colored silk, creating a subtle, elegant effect. This tallit felt like my own skin the instant I enveloped myself in it. I did not want to take it off; that was how good it felt.

Surely the two-year search had been worth it. And how I had evolved during that period! There is no doubt in my mind that through my daily practice, growing awareness, and unrelenting search, I had finally earned the right to wear tzitzit.

**Rabbi Judith Edelstein**, a resident of Manhattan, is Director of Religious Life for the Jewish Home and Hospital Lifecare System. She is also chair of the Board of Directors of the Academy for Jewish Religion; and a member of the Association of Rabbis and Cantors, and the National Association of Jewish Chaplains. She is a candidate for a doctor of ministry degree at Hebrew Union College–Jewish Institute of Religion.

# A Tallit (or Two) to Call My Own

*Sharon Barkauskas*

All around me, women were wearing tallitot. I wondered, what would donning a tallit mean for me? This question gnawed at me through the years.

Growing up in Conservative Judaism, where only the men wore tallitot, this seemed to me to be an exclusively male ritual. However, as time passed and I watched women standing in shul and saying the blessing before wrapping themselves in their own tallitot, I found myself feeling at once jealous and intrigued at the idea of joining with them in this age-old ritual practice.

Another thought crossed my mind as I agonized over whether or when to embark on this next step in my spiritual and educational journey. I was concerned that donning a tallit would be making a "feminist" statement, and I wasn't comfortable with that notion. So, again, I tucked away the thought without taking action.

When I was Bat Mitzvah age, back in the '60s, girls not only did not wear tallitot, but they did not even have a Bat Mitzvah in my hometown of Dover, New Jersey. Because this was the custom, I never felt left out of this life-cycle event.

Sometime later, after both my children became b'nai mitzvah, the sixth- and seventh-graders at my synagogue were making their own tallitot at a Hebrew school workshop. I was in the building at the time, and couldn't help but notice how creative and beautiful the tallitot they were making were, and how much pleasure the children—both boys and girls—were getting from this experience. Again, I felt a little jealous. Later that day, I asked the Hebrew school director if I could purchase a tallit kit for myself, thinking that I would have it on hand when I was ready.

The kit sat on my dining room table for months, until one day I felt it calling out to me to open it up and see what I could make. After a short time, I had designed a simple, but elegant, tallit, tied on the fringes, and put my Hebrew name, Sarah bat Herschel, on one of the corners. In the center was a dove, which holds very special meaning to me. A beautiful dove had flown by my window during a very bleak time in my life, and I had taken it as a sign from God that things would work out okay. The dove has remained a cherished symbol to me from then on, so I incorporated it into my tallit. It was so beautiful!

You would think that I would be anxious to wear it, but it actually took me quite a while before I had the courage to take it out in shul and say the blessing before adorning myself with my beautiful tallit. I carried it with me to services for a few months, but was unable to take the next step. During the High Holy Days that year, a friend who knew I had it with me gave me the encouragement I needed, and that day I stood up, said the blessing, and wrapped myself in my tallit with pride and joy! It was a bit uncomfortable at first, but now I love it and feel so blessed whenever I put it on. I find it brings me closer to God than ever before. I also feel more connected to the community as all of us daven in shul, each with our own tallit.

Recently, I became a bat mitzvah, along with eleven other wonderful women. All of us are on our own individual spiritual and educational journeys, and my Bat Mitzvah was another step in that journey. On the occasion of my Bat Mitzvah, my husband and best friend presented me with a new tallit, one that I had been admiring in the synagogue Judaica shop for a long time. Now I have two beautiful tallitot and have to decide which one to wear on Shabbat. Each of these tallitot makes me feel very special, part of a wonderful tradition and ritual, and wrapped in the love of God.

**Sharon Barkauskas** is a member of Morristown (NJ) Jewish Center–Beit Yisrael, past Sisterhood president of Adath Shalom Synagogue in Parsippany, New Jersey, and an active member of the Women's League for Conservative Judaism. She and her husband Richard have two college-aged children, Brian and Abby.

# What My Tallit Means to Me

*Sara Shapiro-Plevan*

M any years ago, I decided that I wanted to learn how to tie tzitzit. I did it mostly because I wanted to teach my students how to do it, hoping that if they made their own tallitot they would be more inclined to wear them regularly. Over the years, I was lucky enough to help others learn how to tie tzitzit at adult education workshops and programs with students becoming bar and bat mitzvah. I tied tzitzit for others and helped them to design personal, unique tallitot.

Last year, a number of mothers of upcoming b'nai mitzvah began to discuss making tallitot for their children. I helped them shop for fabric, gave hemming and fringe-making instructions, and taught them how to tie tzitzit. These mothers made a very powerful choice to contribute to their child's coming of age in a meaningful way by making tallitot for them and tying their tzitzit for them. I can think of few things more stirring than knowing that young people will take their first steps as adult Jews in a ritual garment made for them by their parents.

As I discussed with these parents the dimensions of the fabric, the appropriate sizes for their children, the history of the tallit, and the meaning of the tzitzit, I found myself carried away. I did not own a tallit. I thought that I was "not quite ready" to take on the mitzvah of wearing a tallit when I pray. I found myself concerned with needing to remember to bring it with me when I go to services, concerned about the cumbersome nature of the garment, and sometimes even concerned about something as shallow as how it would look on me.

Would I throw it over my shoulders "correctly"? Would I feel awkward? But I was tremendously inspired by these parents who wanted to give the gift of the mitzvot to their children, and so I decided to give up my own misgivings and anxieties.

Kol Nidre 5764 (2004) marked the first time I wore my tallit. Now I wear it as regularly as I can.

Making my tallit was certainly challenging: from picking out the right fabric—I think I picked something that will wrinkle too easily—to determining the appropriate dimensions for one's height and armspan (I think mine might be too big!). But I have tied the tzitzit, and I am going to wear it. It is a lovely off-white silk, with a periwinkle atarah and corners. The tzitzit are too long but they remind me of the personal, handcrafted nature of my own tallit, especially when I accidentally get caught up in them at shul. I had wanted to use tzitzit with *techelet* (a thread of blue), but after I purchased the *techelet*, I found that it rubbed off onto the body of the tallit and nearly stained it, so I chose all white instead. Tying the tzitzit had new meaning for me when I did it myself: It wasn't just a "how-to" for others or a complicated art project but something in which I could personally take pride.

I had the entire thing sewn by the Chinese tailor at my dry cleaner: He had no idea what I wanted, so I brought a tallit from my synagogue as a template. When I showed him the template, he said, without prompting, "For praying." The symbol is far from a universal one, but I was touched that he knew and shared his knowledge with me. Much to my dismay, he put the atarah on a bit off-center, but instead of taking it back and having the fabric ripped apart and reconstructed, I try to think of it as adding a bit of character! From under my tallit, I daven in a community of my students who are also getting used to their own new tallitot, each with flaws that make them personal and unique, and we learn the moves together.

I became bat mitzvah wearing my grandfather's tallit: He died many years before I was born, and I was named for him. I was married under a chuppah that was made from my great-grandfather's tallit, which he brought with him from Russia when he came to the United States. Tallitot are ritual symbols of our commitment to mitzvot and to honoring our Jewish tradition: They can also be a highly personal link to our own Jewish experience, and can help us to find our way to renewed personal connection and individual Jewish meaning. I know that personally now, not just because I taught this mitzvah to others but also because I myself wear the fulfillment of this mitzvah and the reminder of all mitzvot around my shoulders.

**Sara Shapiro-Plevan** is the Education Director at Congregation Habonim on Manhattan's Upper West Side, and is currently pursuing an EdD at the William Davidson School of Education at the Jewish Theological Seminary. Ms. Shapiro-Plevan serves on the board of the Jewish Educators' Assembly and MATAN, and is the former chair of the Metropolitan Educators Council of New York. She and her husband, Rabbi William Plevan, and their son Ariel live in Manhattan.

# As Natural as Breathing

*Rabbi Elyse Wechterman*

Taking on the mitzvah of wearing a tallit was as natural as breathing. Not so with other mitzvot—kippot, tefillin, regular prayer. Many of those felt foreign and male. But a tallit—with its wings of protection and its ability to turn any space into a private shelter with the flick of a wrist—how subtle, how comforting, how feminine, how me.

So it was no surprise that my husband's wedding gift to me was the largest, most colorful tallit I have ever seen. We used it first as our chuppah: It had enough room for our dearest friends and family to stand with us as we entered marriage together.

This tallit—too big to be worn regularly—came out again for our son's *brit atifah*, welcoming ceremony. He was wrapped in its protecting layers by designated friends and family as we blessed him with his new name, Avinoam Shalom.

I became a rabbi in this tallit, this time placed on my shoulders by two trusted and dear teachers—my rabbis.

This tallit will come out again as we prepare to welcome our new adopted daughter, Shira Eliana, into our family and into our people with a covenant ceremony that will most surely feature this familiar, and now stained cloth.

I keep fantasizing that I will have the time to needlepoint our family's life-cycle moments and dates near the atarah. Maybe I'll get around to it before my son uses it as his chuppah.

**Rabbi Elyse Wechterman** is the spiritual leader of Congregation Agudas Achim in Attleboro, Massachusetts.

# "Ouch," Said the Torah, or the Power of the Tallit

*Susan Marx*

"Ouch," said the Torah as the wood cracked. A few years ago, the Torah broke while I was helping to dress it on the bimah. The wooden pole around which the parchment scroll is wrapped (called the *etz hayim*) broke. *Ouch* was the sound I seemed to hear.

Cantor Riki (Cantor Erica Lippitz at Congregation Oheb Shalom in South Orange, New Jersey) immediately wrapped a tallit around it. How wonderful, I thought. The tallit will help the Torah. The tallit will comfort the Torah until it is repaired. When I later told this to the cantor, she said she had only covered it with the tallit because the Torah always needs two covers, and the tallit just happened to be there. It could have been covered with anything. But, she commented to me, what a lovely modern midrash.

I began wearing a tallit very recently. When I grew up, a tallit was something a man wore, not a woman. In the summer of 2001, I was in Jerusalem and, while visiting the "cardo," the ancient marketplace in the Jewish Quarter of the Old City, I saw a beautiful tallit with a view of Jerusalem woven in it. The tallit looked at me and said: "Wear me and you will always remember Jerusalem. Try it. Wear me and see what happens to you." And I knew that tallit was meant for me.

God's protective presence, the *Shechinah*, is around us all the time. But when I am wearing my tallit, I am reminded of God's presence. I enjoy being wrapped in it, *l'hetatayf b'tzitzit* (to wrap ourselves in the fringes), as I place my tallit over my head when I say the *Amidah*. It is as if I have created a private sacred space for me alone among the community of worshipers around me. Here I can speak to God directly. It feels like I am wearing protective emotional armor against the often cruel world outside.

So, just as the tallit "protected" the broken Torah, it also helps comfort, heal, and protect me, Sarah Bat Avraham HaLevi ve Beila Rivka, also known as Susan.

**Susan Marx**, who lives in Orange, New Jersey, is an active member of Oheb Shalom, a Conservative congregation in South Orange. She works as an Administrative Assistant for the Jewish National Fund and is also an impressionist painter. She once lived in Jerusalem, and while there worked on the *Encyclopedia Judaica* in the illustrations department.

# An Invincibility Cloak

*Sandra C. Sussman*

*[Editor's Note: The author of this piece read it aloud at the Bar Mitzvah of her best friend's eldest child when she presented him with his tallit at the start of the service. The author has a very close relationship with the young man, Sam, because she lived with Sam's parents in a communal house from long before Sam was born until he was four-and-a-half years old.]*

The tallit, or prayer shawl, is worn by men and women once they have reached their Bar or Bat Mitzvah. And while the fabric may be simple or elaborate, colorful or plain, it is the tzitzit, the fringes on the four corners of the garment, which suffuse it with religious significance. We are commanded to wrap ourselves in tzitzit so that when we look at them we remember to do all the commandments.

A logical question at this point is why does looking at the tzitzit serve as such a reminder? Because the precise and intricate mathematics of strands, wraps, and knots add up to 613, which just happens to be the exact number of mitzvot—commandments—in the Torah. So just to look at the tzitzit is to remember all the commandments, and remembering leads to doing.

Like all effective symbolism, however, the tallit can take on deeper meaning. I encourage you, Sam, to also look upon your tallit as a reminder of all that you've accomplished in this past year. You have surmounted innumerable challenges put before you by your parents and teachers, your family, your friends, and fate. Even more important, you set yourself several formidable tasks and mastered them with an admirable combination of determination and effort.

Harry Potter has an invisibility cloak. I urge you, Sam, to view your tallit as an *invincibility* cloak. When you look upon the tzitzit, be reminded of the commandments; when you look upon the tallit as a whole, be reminded of your deep reservoir of inner strength.

**Sandra C. Sussman** is grateful to the Summer Institutes of the National Havurah Committee for teaching her about the tallit and providing her with a setting where she gained the confidence to wear one herself. She lives and davens (prays) in Princeton, New Jersey, where she has two tallitot (each of which has a story to tell!).

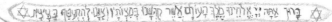

# DREAMWEAVERS: INSPIRED BY DESIGN

A tallit is one of geometry's simples shapes—a rectangle. Graceful fringes at either end lend a fluidity and a sense of movement to the tallit, as they sway in time with davening (praying). But as with many things in life, the tallit is wholly (holy) more than it seems. Whether it's sewn or woven, adorned with embroidery, lace, ribbons, appliqué, or other accents, a tallit—especially one that's handmade—is imbued with spiritual meaning by both the maker and the wearer.

Some contemporary tallitot bear personalized designs that reflect the wearer's name, or feelings about Judaism, or passions in life. Some follow the traditional striped design; others feature rainbow motifs or multicolored abstract elements; still others tell the story of a family within the outlines of the tallit's prescribed shape and other requirements.

In these essays, we find people compelled to fashion tallitot for themselves or for their loved ones. The simple contours of the tallit inspire extraordinary creativity, as paintings on silk express the wearer's devotion to G-d, an *etz hayim* (tree of life) springs from the roots of another's love of Torah, and a mother's love for her daughter and blessings for her future are knit into the very fiber of the tallit. The atarah, or neckpiece, traditionally bears the blessing for the tallit, yet this, too, becomes a way for these tallit-makers to express their deepest spiritual yearnings.

Creating a tallit blends seamlessly with a love of G-d, a love of others, and a dedication to Judaism and its core tenets. None of the tallit-makers whose stories appear here deviated from the biblical mandates in fashioning their tallitot. Yet once they met the requirements for a kosher tallit, their imagination took flight, with images of plants, animals, musical notes, and more that expressed their own wonder at G-d's creation.

—Diana Drew

# The Full Circle Tallit

*Francine Miller*

E veryone at the Temple Beth Sholom Religious School in Chandler, Arizona, was excited about the upcoming Silent Auction. Each class wanted to make something special to show what it had learned that year and to show how much their school meant to them.

Fraidel's class decided to make a tallit that they would donate to the auction. Fraidel, the teacher, purchased the most beautiful white-on-white fabric in the bride's section of the fabric store, and she even splurged on a snow-white fringe the class could sew along the edge.

As work on the tallit progressed, more and more people got involved and more and more people began to fall in love with the prayer shawl. Students from the higher grades stopped by to help the younger children cut and sew, and moms even came to the class to iron and hand-sew where needed.

During one work session, the bobbin on the sewing machine ran out of white thread, so the class decided to use the only other color thread they had that day—turquoise. Yet this slight imperfection only made the tallit more beautiful.

It was a few weeks later, after handling the large tallit many times, that the children asked if they could cut the material in half. A smaller tallit would be easier to work on and more suitable for a lady.

Fraidel was so happy. Now she could have one tallit and donate the other to the auction. Fraidel was joyful because, although she did not realize it, during the creation of the tallit, Fraidel had fallen in love with it and wanted it for her own.

Fraidel imagined far into the future. Maybe after Fraidel had worn the tallit for a few years, she could put it away for a future granddaughter. She dreamed about what her granddaughter's Bat Mitzvah might be like and thought about the ceremony where that very tallit was presented to her beloved grandchild. Fraidel just had to have one of these beautiful tallitot.

Everything would have worked out fine if Fraidel had not made a spur-of-the-moment gift to her sister. There were to be two tallitot—one for the auction and one for Fraidel—but about a month before the auction, Fraidel found out that her sister had been studying Hebrew, in a class of twenty-eight women, for their group Bat Mitzvah. Her sister planned to buy herself a tallit to celebrate the occasion. It was then that Fraidel, in an act of generosity for her dear sister, offered to send her sister the soon-to-be-finished tallit as her Bat Mitzvah gift. Now, once again, there was only one tallit, the twin to the one promised to her sister, but that one was already spoken for: it was destined for the religious school auction.

As completion of the tallit grew near, Fraidel took the long trip into Phoenix to select the religious additions that would make these two tallitot kosher. She purchased two neckpieces containing the prayer written in Hebrew and two sets of long strings, the tzitzit (which are very sacred and have to be tied, knotted, and coiled in a very precise way). Once these items were in place, the tallitot would be finished. However, Fraidel had no idea how she would solve her problem. How could she keep the tallit and also donate it to the auction?

Finally, Fraidel came up with a brilliant plan. Since it was a Silent Auction, Fraidel would just bid on her tallit until she won it! It might cost a bit more than she could afford, but she would pay whatever it cost to outbid anyone else, and she would be victorious and win the prize!

The day arrived! Fraidel entered the auction area before anyone else and placed the prized tallit on the table. Then she got her bidding number, 18, and also bid

$18 (*chai*), which means "life" in Hebrew. At various times throughout the morning, she checked the bidding card. Whoops! Number 8 was also bidding. The price of the tallit was now $24. Fraidel went to $36 (double *chai*). There was more bidding between $36 and $48, so Fraidel decided to go to triple chai, $54. When she returned at noon, with only fifteen more minutes to go until the bidding closed, someone had bid $55. Not wanting to let the tallit slip through her fingers for a mere dollar, Fraidel raised her bid to $56.

Although Fraidel wanted that tallit desperately, although she felt she deserved it because it had been her creation, interest, and passion for several months, she thought about the other bidder. Perhaps it was the parent of one of her students who also had worked on and developed a love for that tallit.

Fraidel left the bidding area. She turned the fate of the tallit over to God. Fraidel had bid triple chai plus two. If the tallit were to be hers, God would decide!

After the bidding closed, Faidel returned to the auction to find out if she had won the valued prize. There, holding the tallit, was the mother of one of her students. Her daughter was in Fraidel's class. The bidding was over and the mom had won the beautiful tallit!

The mom looked at Fraidel in astonishment. "Were you the other bidder?" she asked. As Fraidel tearfully nodded, the mother handed Fraidel the tallit and said, "I bought it for you!"

*Epilogue*: Two-and-a-half years later, as Fraidel attended the Bat Mitzvah of bidder number 8's daughter, she found out that number 8 was part of the 2003 adult B'nai Mitzvah class. Fraidel asked number 8 if she could honor her, and the event, by making a duplicate tallit for her. On May 3, 2003, during the morning Shabbat service, Fraidel presented a tallit to Jennifer (number 8). The tallit mitzvah had come full circle.

**Francine Miller** is a retired public high school English teacher who also spent ten years teaching religious school at Temple Beth Sholom in Chandler, Arizona. She lives in Mesa, Arizona, with her husband, Paul, a retired auditor. They have two adult children.

# Shoshannah's Tallit

## Paula Barber

Some projects are beshert—they just happen to find you and you just happen to find them. I did not plan to create a tallit for my daughter, Shoshannah, but always hoped that she would take on the obligation of wearing one. I started wearing a tallit just before her eldest brother's Bar Mitzvah, and felt it added spiritual depth and a distinctly different dimension to my experience during services.

Though of feminist inclination, I did not take on the wearing of the tallit as a feminist statement. I was not interested in mimicking what men do and wear in order to assert my "equality." What I sought was personal: a ritual catalyst to the spiritual connection of prayer.

Wearing a tallit creates a holy boundary between everyday experience and the experience of prayer. In separating myself from all the ordinary activities of daily living, I have a heightened receptiveness and sensitivity to God's presence. I wanted Shoshannah to feel this prayer experience, this focused connection with *Hashem*; to do so, her undistracted presence in mind, body, and spirit was essential.

ALL OF THIS was in my mind when, about a year and a half before Shoshannah's Bat Mitzvah, I was wandering through the yarn aisle at a craft store and noticed a yarn that appealed to me. The yarn was a soft, off-white cotton with a speckling of spring colors, which made me think of the spring season of Shoshannah's upcoming Bat Mitzvah. I thought the yarn would make a lovely tallit for Shoshannah because of its colors and comfortable feel. Not certain of how much yarn would be needed, I bought all the skeins of yarn in that dye lot. I could have made two or three tallitot from that quantity of yarn. As I leafed through some booklets for knitted afghans, I found a pattern that I thought would be just right for the body of the tallit.

There had to be something *beshert* about my creating this tallit for Shoshannah because my knitting skills were certainly no match for the task that lay before me. I had dreamed of a design that would wrap my daughter in blessings, but I had only a limited practical strategy for carrying out my plan. After a couple of weeks of struggling unsuccessfully with the directions and producing some pretty but strange-looking lengths of knitting, I decided that I needed some assistance in designing and crafting the tallit. I realized, at this point, that I wasn't going to be able to finish it on my own.

Fortunately, I brought the project with me to a family function, and my cousin's wife and another cousin's close friend—both very talented knitters—came to my rescue. They helped me adapt the pattern for the tallit into reasonable proportions, and then taught me to keep track of the stitches so my knitting produced the desired result. Still, there was a lot of knitting and ripping before I had something resembling the pattern in the book.

The tallit project then became my constant companion whenever I had to sit and wait. This was truly a blessing, as waiting has never been one of my strengths. Over the coming months, I knitted while I waited for my mother to come out of surgery, when I watched Shoshannah's softball games, during Shoshannah's cello practice, during long car rides, when I waited for someone but did not have enough time to leave and accomplish any of the myriad tasks that populate my to-do list. Though fairly observant, but not *shomer Shabbat*, I never knitted or worked on the tallit on Shabbat, as much as I longed to occupy my hands to fill the time.

As I KNITTED the tallit, I meditated; I prayed and blessed every stitch. I thought about Shoshannah, about God, about our role in the world, about what it meant to be a contemporary Jewish woman and what kind of Jewish woman I hoped Shoshannah would become. I reflected about how blessed our family was to have Shoshannah in our midst: how her kindness draws others to her like magnetism, how her way is understated, yet confident— quite remarkable for one who is on the cusp of woman- hood. I knew there would be challenges ahead for her, but I hoped that wrapping herself in her tallit on Shabbat and during the holidays would somehow sustain Shoshannah, as it does me.

The time had finally come when the tallit was the right length. Shoshannah and I measured it against my tallit and it was the just the right size in both length and width. I washed the tallit to prepare it for sewing on the atarah (collar) and corners, and all the blue flecks disap- peared from the last several skeins of yarn used to knit the tallit. I washed replacement skeins of yarn to make sure the dye was not going to wash out, ripped out the defective section, and continued to knit. I wasn't upset about doing the replacement knitting; I had gotten attached to working on the tallit and had mixed feelings about finishing this project.

A trip to the fabric store produced the perfect match- ing colors for the material for the atarah and corners. I hoped I would be able to embroider the names of the matriarchs in the corners and our family's names on the inside. Shoshannah wanted the blessing for putting on the tallit embroidered on the atarah. Once again, I hit a snag: The silky, soft, crushed velvet material we had cho- sen for the atarah was also very stretchy, and did not allow for any type of embroidery or crewel work. One particularly discouraging evening, Shoshannah said that she would prefer a "normal" woman's tallit to the one I had been so painstakingly creating for her. I asked her to be patient, that I had one last idea, and if that didn't work, we'd make the knitted tallit into an afghan and buy a ready-made one for her. A trip to the craft store yielded a lovely pre-made gold braiding that gave the tallit the finished look it needed. Shoshannah was pleased, and I was relieved that all my effort had produced something she would feel comfortable wearing.

The next challenge was to find tzitzit that were not made from wool, as both Shoshannah and I get a pretty bad case of the "itchies" from wool. One of the managers of our synagogue's sisterhood gift shop found rayon tzitzit and ordered them for us. The tzitzit that arrived were extremely bright white and looked unnatural next to the tallit. I made a cup of strong tea, set the tzitzit in the tea as a dye, rinsed them well, and then they matched the tallit very nicely. While they dried, we made sure they were behind a closed door so our cats would not be tempted to add their sense of adventure to the last stages of the tallit project.

I had hoped to have our rabbi assist us in tying the knots on the tzitzit, but he was unavailable on the night we had planned. By his design or God's, we'll never know, but Shoshannah and I set out to complete this last task together. Our synagogue administrator said she had made her son's tallit and that the directions for tying the knots on the tzitzit were not difficult to follow. I found directions for tying tzitzit in Strassfeld's *Jewish Family Catalog*. Shoshannah decided she wanted to tie the knots herself, but she reserved the last one for me.

At our dining room table, we sat together, me counting, she tying the knots, both counting our blessings to get to the point of my completion and the point of her beginning. When the tallit was finished, we performed the ritual of biting off of the ends of the strings. (Actually, though we tried, we really could not bite through the rayon, so we used a scissors.) When the tzitzit was completed, I placed the tallit on Shoshannah's shoulders and together we recited the *Shehecheyanu* prayer for new beginnings. Creating Shoshannah's tallit for her Bat Mitzvah provided an ending and a beginning that bound us together and to *Hashem*.

As her Bat Mitzvah approached, I yearned to wrap Shoshannah in blessings, to create the means for her to find sacred space and spiritual connection. I sought to assist in her spiritual development. I wanted her to feel my enduring love when she wrapped herself in her tallit to pray. She is part of my connection to God through the next generation, and I am her link to her heritage from the past. I am hopeful that her connection to God will bring her peace and happiness and she will continue to wrap herself in the way of mitzvot.

During the Friday night services before Shoshannah's Bat Mitzvah, as I placed the tallit on her shoulders, I spoke of my knitting blessings into the fabric and of my hopes that she would wear her tallit often and wear it well. The tallitot and the choices in how to make spiritual connection are now hers.

**Paula Barber** and her husband, Howard Buxbaum, have three children, Shoshannah, 14, Joseph, 19, and Jacob, 21. Ms. Barber is a member of Morristown (NJ) Jewish Center–Beit Yisrael and a founding member of the Burnham Park Minyan, a havurah that has been in existence for over fourteen years. She is also a social worker specializing in geriatrics.

# The Hebrew School Project
## Muriel Hertan

Never before had the synagogue been so divided. Well, the parents of the after-school Hebrew school anyway. They either loved her or they hated her. We loved her. To us she was a gift from heaven. Not one of the three children we sent to Hebrew school had ever wanted to go. The complaints went from "I'm missing soccer practice" to "I'm never going to get my real homework done" or "Why do I have to be here? I don't believe in G-d." But this fourth child, our baby, was different. Sure, the first few years she had her complaints, just like her siblings, but not this year. What changed her attitude was, plain and simple, the teacher.

Here was a woman of understanding and compassion, one who was steeped in the educational philosophy that the way children learn is to make them part of the process. According to those who didn't like her, she wasted time in the classroom when the youngsters could be learning more in a traditional manner.

How would their kids ever be properly prepared for their B'nai Mitzvah?

First there was the business of the Shabbat debate. The teacher divided the class in two and assigned them to do research on the do's and don'ts of Shabbat observance. What was all this about making lists of positives and negatives, the things we are permitted to do and the things we should not do on the Sabbath according to Conservative laws of observance? Then she wasted even more time having the children practice for a debate as to whether or not these laws should be changed to accommodate modern times. In all the years that children attended after-school Hebrew school at our synagogue, we never saw the commitment, enthusiasm, knowledge, and delight in the youngsters about the Sabbath that we saw during that memorable debate and afterwards.

So what was all this talk about cloth? The teacher was using class time to instruct and guide the children in making a tallit? She set out to show them that it wasn't just a piece of cloth we threw over our shoulders when in synagogue. She was determined to dispel the myth that shuls in Europe were not heated and the men needed some other piece of clothing to keep them warm as they prayed. A tallit, after all, had purpose and meaning.

For us, first came the shopping for the cloth. My daughter and I visited every store that carried fabric and she looked at all the merchandise they had to offer. Her little fingers touched and petted the myriad offerings and at long last she settled on a light blue denim. I was taken aback by her selection and asked her to consider whether this fabric was too casual for the intended purpose. She was insistent and persistent, so the denim was purchased and lovingly carried home.

In the classroom, the first part of the project went quickly, as it was only measuring and cutting the rectangle whose purpose it is to hold the tzitzit, or fringes, that would adorn each corner. Next came the application of the neckband, which carried the blessing that is said every time the tallit is placed on the shoulders of the wearer. Usually the neckband is embroidered, but for this project the children wrote theirs in indelible ink. Anyone peeking in the classroom window would wonder at the sight of the young heads studiously bent over as they stitched the hem of the rectangle or affixed the neckband. Little hands were busy at the task and even the boys were serious about making neat and even stitches with their needles.

It was Moses who brought the Lord's message that the Jewish people were to wear on their garments fringes that had a cord of blue to help them recall His commandments and to observe them. Our daughter's class was now embarking on the most important part of the project—tying the tzitzit at the corners of this authentically Jewish garment.

Making the fringes is, in reality, a form of macramé, and it requires a great deal of coordination. The classmates helped each other with all the prescribed strands and knots. There are specific regulations for the circles that surround the strands and the pattern that is made. The concentration of each child was amazing. They put all their love and caring into the counting and the turning and the knotting. No store-bought tallitot could compare to the construction of those handmade in this classroom.

In addition to discovering for themselves what went into making a tallit, the children asked many questions about who could wear it and when. They were delighted to learn that girls could don a tallit as well as boys. In fact, the boys had to wait until they were thirteen, but girls—because they may become bat mitzvah at twelve—could put one on at that age. The rituals of kissing the Torah with the fringes and honoring the tallit as a religious article by never taking it into a bathroom all figured in the conversation of the working learners. During one discussion, the class came to the unanimous agreement that among the best times they have in synagogue is when they play with the fringes of their dads' tallitot.

As this project proceeded, our daughter couldn't wait to leave "real" school and get to Hebrew class. The tallit she was making was the topic of conversation many evenings at the dinner table. At long last, the day came when she brought home the completed tallit. It was cause for much celebration. There were looks of surprise and envy on the faces of her siblings. For the first time ever, our baby took all the comments in stride as she presented the tallit to her father. I shall never forget the expression on her face. It absolutely shone with contentment and delight. I do believe she actually grew in stature as the smile stretched clear across from ear to ear.

That expression was but a prelude to the one our

daughter displayed that Saturday morning when her dad took the denim tallit out of his tallit bag and put it on for services. Every time he wore it, it elicited comments from those sitting near him. I don't know who enjoyed those words more—he or she.

The most important wearing of the tallit and, unfortunately, its last, was when it was placed around the shoulders of her dad as he lay in his casket. There was never a question among her siblings that Dad would be buried in this tallit. Once again, through her tears, my daughter's face shone at the thought that a little bit of her would be with her father forever.

**Muriel Hertan**, who lives in Monroe Township, New Jersey, is a retired teacher. She volunteers with a group of senior immigrants who just became or want to become citizens. A lifelong member of Women's American ORT, she now serves as that organization's national representative to the non-governmental organizations (NGOs) at the United Nations. She is still a member in good standing at the Commack (NY) Jewish Center on Long Island.

# A Tallit Wrapped in Memories

*Rosanne Bornstein*

several years ago, my sister Sandi was diagnosed
with metastasized breast cancer after twelve years
of wishing, hoping and praying that the cancer was
gone. In order to help me deal with this tragedy, I began
going to a learners' minyan at Congregation Agudath
Israel in Caldwell, New Jersey. A rabbinical student,
Paula Mack-Drill, led the minyan.

The journey that started here was a great support as
Sandi and I dealt with her illness. As her world became
smaller and smaller, she and I talked about the learning
that I was experiencing, and the spiritual lessons I was
drawing from the minyan. Sandi lived in Texas, two
hours away from her synagogue, so she loved to hear
about my learning. Through that sharing we became
connected in a totally new way. The depth of our conversations and the new understanding of our lives and our
souls that we gained from these conversations were
amazing to both of us.

Before Sandi died, I visited her in Texas and she gave
me a hand-painted robe that she loved. It hung on the
back of my closet door for months. Then, about four
months after she died, I began working with Paula on
ways to mourn and celebrate Sandi's life. As I began to
get a grip on the changes my relationship with Sandi had
brought to my life, I realized that I could always feel that
connection to Sandi by honoring her life with a tallit
made from her precious robe.

I needlepointed the atarah and included my Hebrew
name. The needlepoint included doves and stars in

strong beautiful colors, highlighted with gold thread. The corners represented a heart, a hand, a head, and a ladder, which are all symbols used by Rabbi Alan Silverstein in his sermons and teaching. The needlepoint was attached to a length of fabric from the robe's sleeve.

Whenever I wrap myself in this tallit, I feel hugged by Sandi. As much as I mourn her death, I celebrate the new awareness that I have achieved and continue to experience those joys that she brought to my life.

**Rosanne Bornstein** and her husband Ira live in Verona, New Jersey, and have two grown children, Jason and Gayle. Ms. Bornstein, who has worked in education for twenty years, also volunteers as the Grant Coordinator for the Verona Municipal Alliance Committee. The family belongs to Congregation Agudath Israel in Caldwell, New Jersey, where they participate in many of the spiritual learners' groups.

# The Tallit We Invited to My Daughter's Bat Mitzvah

*Lori Cohen*

Most girls become a bat mitzvah in seventh grade. Amy's birthday is at the end of the year, so she had to wait until eighth grade to turn thirteen. That was no problem for her. She was used to being the youngest, waiting her turn, watching while others seemed to grow older faster. She was in no hurry to grow up and that was just fine with me. Amy is creative and proud to express her individuality, not because she needs to make a statement, but because she isn't afraid to be herself. We didn't want a cookie-cutter Bat Mitzvah; we wanted it to mean something.

Party after party, we wondered where the mitzvah was in *Bat Mitzvah*. We knew we weren't interested in keeping up with the Schwartzes, but even the least extravagant extravaganzas seemed to feel empty. Why is this party different from all others?

We wanted this milestone in all our lives to feel significant and Jewish. We sorted through all the elements of the experience and realized that the process was going to be as important as the product. This led us to the tallit.

We looked through catalogs and stores, searching for a tallit for Amy's special day. After seeing the same ones over and over again, we realized that Amy's tallit should really feel like her own. Thinking back over years of costumes we had created together, we figured that if we could sew a lobster, a pizza, and a mermaid, we should be able to handle a rectangle-shaped tallit. The excitement was palpable, the possibilities endless.

Our questions started flying. How do you make a tallit? What are the rules? How could we find directions? Whom could we ask? These queries felt much more comfortable to us than Where should we have the party? What kind of music should we have? What will we wear? We knew we were thinking about a truly important part of the Bat Mitzvah.

The research began with our rabbi. Of course we can make the tallit, she assured us. Why not? We read books and went to visit a woman in our congregation who makes tallitot. She was helpful, but it felt like getting a recipe with an important ingredient left out. Perhaps that element was time. After digesting all the information, we were ready to begin.

The first step was to choose the fabric. I presented Amy with a bag of old handkerchiefs I had been saving. They were brightly colored squares that had been used by my mother and grandmother in an era when no woman would be without a hankie. Amy was intrigued by the beautiful fabrics and the idea that her ancestors could be so vividly represented in the present by these tiny bits of the past.

After deciding to use the handkerchiefs for Amy's tallit, everything seemed to flow. We went to the local fabric store and settled on a mediocre piece of white fabric. We knew it wasn't perfect, but it didn't matter. The idea of creating a meaningful tallit was all we felt we needed. It was quickly decided that we would cut the handkerchiefs into Jewish stars to appliqué onto the plain white base; larger stars for the body and smaller ones for the atarah. Amy sorted the fabrics and decided how to place each one. She loved the tiny flowers, the one with the little girl on it, and the purple one that was so well worn it was hard to sew. It was as if we were having a dialog with our ancestors and they were guiding us on this journey. Amy added pieces from my prom dress, my father's handkerchief, and my husband's father's tie.

Heart-shaped pieces provided reinforcement for the tzitzit and referenced Amy's Hebrew name, Ahava (love).

It took months of cutting and sewing to make Amy's tallit. She would be chanting her Torah portion and I would be sewing. I would be cooking dinner and she would be sewing. Sometimes we thought we were crazy. Everyone else went to the store, purchased a tallit, and that was the end of it. We seemed to be reinventing the wheel, and it felt just as important.

Many elements of Amy's Bat Mitzvah were not ordinary. We made tie-dyed kippot and took all our guests to a Catskills resort for a sleepover. The arrangements on the bimah were baskets of toys we donated to a children's hospital, and guests read books on tape that we sent to needy kids. Amy worked hard and did a beautiful job in every way. We truly found many ways to put the mitzvah into her Bat Mitzvah.

When I think about her coming of age, I always feel that the most important part was the creation of her tallit. She is eighteen now, and has created many wonderful memories for me. One of the most precious is the tallit we made together for her Bat Mitzvah.

**Lori Cohen** is Youth Director and Early Childhood Center Director at Temple Israel of Northern Westchester, in Croton, New York.

# A Tale of Two Tallitot

### Shirley Musikant

I have two daughters who came of age when Bat Mitzvah was not yet the custom. However, they both had good Hebrew school educations and have kept up synagogue affiliation into the present. Both are active members in their own congregations—one Reform, the other Conservative.

After her first child was born, my younger daughter, Laurie, joined a B'nai Mitzvah class. At the time of her becoming a bat mitzvah, I had a beautiful Battenberg lace kippah made for her by a friend of mine. A few years later, I asked the same friend if she could make a tallit for my daughter. She told me to get the material and she would make one. She suggested going to antiques shops that specialized in old linens and recommended a runner or a tablecloth—anything that had possibilities.

I remembered that I had a tablecloth given to me years ago by a sweet aunt of mine. It was made of fine cotton with hand embroidery—I think the technique is called cutwork. The cloth was off-white, probably from age; the embroidery was all of one color—a soft gray/beige. It was cut to size, incorporating the design to good advantage. I made fringes along the two short ends. My friend attached the atarah (an imported piece of tapestry ribbon, about three inches wide) and tied the four corner tzizit according to prescribed tradition.

Laurie wore it proudly: It was unique and it had a history. When a congregant remarked that it reminded her of a tablecloth, she felt very self-conscious and no longer comfortable wearing it to Sabbath services, until I pointed out to her that her tallit was a symbol of the changing role of Jewish women. From table to bimah, from tablecloth to tallit in one short generation. Not only was her tallit one-of-a-kind, it had a history and symbolic meaning.

Laurie and her husband are both psychiatrists. Together they are raising two fine children, creating a Jewish home, and taking their place in synagogue life and the Jewish community near Boston.

Laurie's tallit was one of a kind for only a few years. My elder daughter, Ellie, followed suit. She embarked on a two-year course of study leading to her becoming a bat mitzvah. Another tallit was made from the tablecloth. A different piece of tapestry ribbon was found to fashion the atarah on her tallit. So the two tallitot are twins, but not identical.

Ellie is a gifted, professional storyteller. Her husband is a sociologist who teaches and leads research at Columbia University. Both are active in their synagogue. Their two children are college graduates and are out in the working world.

I've often wondered what my Tante Sonia would think of what I did to her tablecloth, which she gave me as a gift. Somehow, I think she'd be pleased, especially if she had seen Laurie and Ellie standing side by side on the bimah, wearing pieces of her tablecloth as tallitot, on the occasion of Laurie's daughter, Sonia, becoming a bat mitzvah.

**Shirley Musikant** lives in Verona, New Jersey, near her daughter Ellie. She retired from a career as an elementary school counselor. She has three children and six grandchildren. (Her eldest child is a son. She did not have his tallit made.)

# Louis's Tallit

*Deborah Green*

When my grandson Louis asked me to make a tallit for his upcoming Bar Mitzvah, I was delighted—and then I panicked. His Bar Mitzvah was less than six weeks away and although I am a quilter, I had never made a tallit before. I had, however, explored the idea in passing, and knew there were a few rules and guidelines: The fabric must not be a mixture of wool and linen; a neckpiece, or atarah, was necessary, since a tallit is considered a garment and should not be worn inside-out or upside-down; and it must have tzitzit tied into 613 knots.

Louis had made two other requests. First, the tallit should be made of silk, because he felt that wool would be too warm; and second, it should be white or off-white.

I spent several days designing the appliqué for the tallit. Since Louis's Hebrew name is Arieh, I knew I would want lions. (*Ari* is the Hebrew word for lion.) And, since this would be the first, but hopefully not the last, time he would be reading from the Torah, I knew I wanted to incorporate a Torah scroll into the design. Although Louis would read from only one passage on his Bar Mitzvah, I wanted the lesson of his tallit to be that the entire Torah is important, and that he is its guardian and it is also his.

I looked through all the books of Jewish design I could find, because my drawing skills are sadly lacking.

When I found the lion I wanted, he was crouched and I wanted him leaping, so I traced him in stages, rising from the crouched position to the angle I liked, and used a copier to make him the right size. Next, I found a wonderful woodcut of an open Torah scroll, and adapted that design for an appliqué between two lions.

What to put on the scroll? I found inspiration in yet another book of Jewish designs. I used a bet, for *bereshit*, the first letter of the first word in the Torah and a lamed for the last letter of the last word in the Torah, *yisrael*.

With the design done, I was off to the fabric store, where it seemed just the right silks were waiting for me. I found an off-white silk for the body of the tallit itself and a deep navy for the appliqué background. Then I spotted a wonderful fabric made of multitoned gold silk patchwork squares (just the thing to set a quilter's heart aflutter). The squares could be cut apart and used as the reinforcement squares for the tzitzit corners; and cut in a strip to be used for the atarah.

The next stop was a Judaica shop for a tzitzit kit and an instruction book for tying. I wanted the tallit be a present from my husband as well, and tying the knots was to be his responsibility. After years of tying knots for our various boats, I knew he was up to the challenge.

The making of the tallit, its embroidery and appliqué, took many hours and was a joyful experience. I said a *Shehecheyanu* when I finished, and handed the tallit off to my husband for the tzitzit.

The look on Louis's face when we gave him his tallit told me all I needed to know. He was thrilled. I gave it to him two weeks before his Bar Mitzvah, on Simchat Torah. Somehow the timing seemed right.

This might have been the first tallit I made, but I know it will not be the last. I have five other grandchildren, and several other family members, including my son, have dropped not-so-subtle hints to put them on my tallit-making "list." I believe each of these tallitot will be "born" when I have a clear message for the design. It is not enough, I think, just to make a beautiful fringed shawl: Each tallit needs its own dvar Torah.

**Deborah Green** and her husband of forty-six years live in Fair Haven, New Jersey, and are members of Congregation B'nai Israel in Rumson, New Jersey. She is president of her quilting guild, Rebecca's Reel Quilters of Poricy Park. Mrs. Green is retired several times (from what is now Lucent Technologies and then from her own bridal business). The Greens have three children and six grandchildren, all of whom encourage Mrs. Green in her efforts as a quilter and fabric artist. Currently, she is working on designs for several tallitot for other family members and is in the early stages of a design for a family chuppah.

# Poppa's Tallitot

## *Marilyn Waxman*

Toward the end of his life, my late husband Bertram (Bob), known as "Poppa" to all his grandchildren, had very painful arthritis in his hands. His doctor suggested exercising his fingers so they wouldn't stiffen up. Bob asked me to teach him needlepoint and embroidery: He thought it would be an artistic challenge for him to create tallitot for his grandchildren.

He bought a book that had all the instructions on how to make a tallit. First, the material had to be "kosher" (no mixing of different material types). The rabbi had to approve this choice.

Then he had to learn how to make the tzitzit (the precise way of tying the knots on the ends of the tallit).

Each grandson—Adam, Jared, Jeremy, and Andrew—got to choose the colors for his tallit. Each tallit was personally styled and labeled "By Poppa, with love." Bob also made each grandson original, needlepoint yarmulkes with scenes of Israel, and tallit envelope bags, in which to hold their handmade treasures.

When our grandsons go to religious services, people always admire the tallitot and yarmulkes, and the youngsters say with pride, "My Poppa made it!"

Our son, Stephen, and our son-in-law, Stephen, also received tallitot as gifts from Poppa. Our daughter, Marcy, received a needlepoint work of art celebrating Judaism, which she has framed. It now hangs proudly in her home.

Bob also crocheted one hundred yarmulkes to be given to guests at each Bar and Bat Mitzvah. When our granddaughter, Rachel, became a bat mitzvah, her Poppa made her a beautiful needlepoint Shabbat scene.

Our grandsons are now grown and the tallitot have been used at two of their weddings. One grandson, David, was married in San Diego on a cliff overlooking the ocean. Poppa's tallit was used both as a chuppah, underneath which the couple were married, and as a wrap encircling the couple as they were wed. The other grandson, Adam, had a lovely wedding ceremony in Philadelphia. Poppa's tallit was again used in a sweet emotional manner: The two moms wrapped the tallit around their children as the rabbi declared them as one. At the wedding of our third grandson, Jared, Poppa's tallit again played a prominent role, making this loving grandfather's presence felt through the gift of his tallitot.

**Marilyn Waxman** lived in Union, New Jersey, for thirty-seven years before moving to the Clearbrook Adult Community in Monroe, New Jersey, about twenty years ago. The family belonged to Congregation Beth Shalom in Union, where both she and her husband sang in the shul choir. Today, at eighty-nine, she creates silk floral arrangements for various clients, a pursuit that started as a hobby years ago.

# Shoshana & Her Tallit

## Sherri Roberts

One of the first phrases I learned when my husband Larry and I lived in Israel for three years in the mid-1980s was *Kol hat'chalah kashah*, "Every beginning is difficult." At that time, Larry was a photojournalist working at the University of Haifa, and I was a district health educator with the Israel Ministry of Health office in Nazareth. We lived in Haifa, and that's where we started our family. Unfortunately, health concerns forced us to return to the United States, but I continue to express my love of the Holy Land, and its cultures and peoples, through fiber art, including tallitot, which I've made collaboratively with each of my children as they became b'nai mitzvah.

Over the years, I have learned that we can never predict what will happen to us. But in our youngest daughter Shoshana, who recently became a bat mitzvah, I have seen hints of how, as she grows up and matures, she may overcome uncertainties and determine her own direction.

In third grade she faced a tough Judaics teacher at the Hebrew Academy—me. I didn't pull any punches. When the situation required, I disciplined or praised her along with the rest of the students. Shoshana actually survived the school year with friends intact, excellent grades in both Hebrew and secular studies, and she and I could still relish each other's company.

As she grew older, Shoshana saw how much her brother Chaim had liked studying tae kwon do, and she asked to learn the martial arts discipline herself. She has kept up the routine for several years already and has taught those older than she is, as well as learned from those who are younger. Through tae kwon do she has also focused on setting goals and reaching for them.

Shoshana has gone after other things that were important to her. She wanted to become part of the first violin section in the school orchestra. So she practiced nightly and made it. She may want to become a veterinarian, so she has volunteered as a "Pet Pal" at a local vet for over a year now. She gets up every Sunday at 7:00 a.m., no complaints, no crankiness, and goes to exercise the dogs and cats, clean up after them, and help wherever it is needed.

At her Bat Mitzvah, I noted that I have a tradition of designing each of my children's prayer shawls. When it came time to choose a phrase and images for her tallit, the choices were easy. The phrase "Whatever it is in your power to do, do with all your might" (*Kol asher tim'tzah yadech la'asot b'koch'ch ahseh*) was perfect for her neckpiece. The stylized lion's paw represents making an imprint, having an impact wherever she goes. And the colors of the design blend from one to another and come back around in a cycle.

I am so proud of who Shoshana is and what she has accomplished at such a young age. We were talking about roller coasters one day, and how people react to them. Shoshana said, "I don't see the point to screaming. I just brace myself." I agree. Handle life by not being afraid, grabbing hold, and enjoying the ride! I hope that the tallit I made for her reflects this courage and zest for life, and that it shields her in God's grace as she makes her own way in the world.

**Sherri Roberts** lives in Pittsburgh and has three children. She enjoys creating distinctive tallitot by drawing on the special interests, skills, and family history of the bar or bat mitzvah, and then incorporating into the design visual symbols that express the essence of who the wearer is.

# A Tallit Uniquely My Own
### Rabbi Beverly Weintraub Magidson

In the spring of 1972, I was a junior at Brandeis University, majoring in Near Eastern and Judaic Studies. My interest in ordination had been awakened the year before with the publicity about Sally Priesand (the first woman ordained as a rabbi in the United States), and I had transferred to Brandeis over the summer of 1971 with the goal of entering rabbinical school after graduation.

That year at Brandeis there were several of us Jewish feminists—or at least women interested in exploring their relationship with Judaism with new eyes. We formed a women's minyan in the fall, and often talked about the relationship between the commandments and our lives as young, educated women, unbound by the demands of children.

During the winter, I decided that I wanted to take on the mitzvah of wearing a tallit. But the men's tallitot all looked very masculine to me, and I wanted something that would be uniquely mine. Before I went home for Passover break, I measured the newly purchased "super-Jew" tallit belonging to my boyfriend (now my husband), which did not simply hang around his neck. He could raise the ends up on his shoulders, leaving his arms free. I wanted to be able to do that, too. Richard is quite a bit taller than my four-foot-eleven frame, so I knew mine needed to be smaller than that.

During Passover vacation, I shopped in Hudson's huge store in downtown Detroit, with its wonderful fabric department. There I purchased fabric of light turquoise, with matching satin for the corners, and a wide, brocaded ribbon for the atarah. I also purchased purple velvet for a bag, along with a beautiful multi-colored fabric for the lining. Fortunately, I had learned how to sew while in high school, and had a new sewing machine—a high school graduation gift from my parents. I put the whole thing together, including hand-sewn buttonholes in the corners. The fringes along the edge were white; I took them off my high school graduation tassels (my high school colors being green and white). I carefully threaded the white tassel fringes through small hems at the edges of the tallit.

I don't remember how I got the tzitzit thread, but it was at that point that I realized that I didn't know enough to proceed on my own. So I talked to my father, who had attended cheder in Poland before his immigration to Canada at the age of ten. I really didn't expect him to know very much, but when I asked him what he knew about tying tzitzit, he rattled off the numbers as if he had learned them the day before! He then helped me tie them, instructing me to tie the first knot in such a way that the tzitzit did not hang directly down in the direction of the ground. (Many years later, I discovered that there is a disagreement about that, but my father was certain, so I assume that this was the *minhag* [custom] of his town in Poland.)

I first wore my tallit to a local Conservative synagogue in Detroit, during Yom Tov at the end of Passover. I felt very self-conscious, but very proud. The woman behind me whispered to her husband, "Look, Lenny, a woman with a tallis! A woman with a tallis!" I felt truly dressed for prayer.

I proudly wore this tallit for the next seven years, until I made a new one (this time white, with embroidered ribbons for stripes, and a needlepointed atarah) for ordination. I wore it in Reform, Conservative, and even some Orthodox services—frequently garnering stares or comments. Whatever anyone said (or didn't dare to say), the one thing I knew was that when I wrapped myself for prayer, I wore a tallit that was uniquely mine.

**Rabbi Beverly Weintraub Magidson** was ordained at the Hebrew Union College–Jewish Institute of Religion in 1979 and admitted to the Rabbinical Assembly of America in 1985 as one of the first Conservative women rabbis. She currently is Director of Chaplaincy Services for the United Jewish Federation of Northeastern New York in Albany. She lives with her husband Richard and their two children. She currently uses her first store-bought tallit, but she may go back to making her own.

# The Intricacies
# of Fashioning Tallitot

## Menorah Rotenberg

The story of my tallit is the story of how I began
making tallitot. It begins with acknowledging the
debt I owe to my son Ethan Rotenberg and to his
cousin Rabbi David Golinkin. David, then a rabbinical
student at the Jewish Theological Seminary (and now
president of the Schechter Institute of Jewish Studies in
Jerusalem), taught Ethan how to tie tzitzit when he was
eleven. As soon as Ethan became proficient, he asked me
to buy him material to make a tallit for himself. It was a
very elementary affair, and he could do most of what
was needed himself. But he asked me to embroider his
grosgrain-ribbon atarah with his name. That became one
of the novel and enduring features of all the tallitot I
have made ever since, including one I made for my
daughter's wedding.

After helping Ethan make his tallit, I decided to
make one for myself. I belonged to an egalitarian havurah and our synagogue had just started a bi-monthly
parallel egalitarian service. I felt that instead of taking
my husband's tallit each time I read Torah or led a part
of the service, I should have my own. Since I quilt and
sew, it never occurred to me to buy one. Seeing how easy
it was for Ethan to make his, I thought I could make
mine quickly as well.

How wrong I was. Ethan's took him a week or so;
mine took over a year. The difference was that mine was

an artistic venture, calling upon not only my sewing skills but also a vision of what my tallit should look like and mean. It needed to express who I was because, in many ways, a personalized tallit is always a presentation of self.

Blessed with the name *Menorah*, which I have always loved, I decided to appliqué a huge menorah on the back of my tallit. My inspiration for this was a poster in our dining room that Kopel Gurin had designed for the twentieth anniversary of the State of Israel. The poster had a large appliquéd menorah with lions on each side (on my tallit's lining, I signed my name and I credited him for the design). Thus appliqué was to become another enduring feature of all my tallitot. I chose at least six different-colored fabrics in silky material that would adorn the royal blue ground. Gracing the tops of each branch of the menorah were tuliplike flowers; I decided to fill them with sparkling beads. That led to my use of beads, sequins, and layers of lustrous yarn that I laid down with a couching stitch. My atarah had my name on it, as did Ethan's, but I decided that mine should be my full name when I was called up to the Torah. So I used my mother's name as well as my father's: *Menorah bat Soreh Gittel v'Yechzkeyl*. This too became a feature of all my atarot.

Shortly after I finished my tallit, my elder son, Josiah, was to become bar mitzvah. It was eminently clear to me that I would make his tallit. What is wonderful about the artistic process is the intersection of thoughtfulness and the power of the unconscious. Thus I am not at all clear as to what led me to decide that I would appliqué a verse from either his Torah portion or his Haftarah in huge letters that would, like my menorah, take up almost the entire back of his tallit. The front would have two stripes on each side—as did mine—in a color that matched his atarah and the lining. I felt that the stripes would reflect the traditional striped tallit. The lining that I have backed each tallit with was an artistic decision born of the need to cover all the stitches that showed through the back of the material. I decided on the pattern and then asked an artist friend of mine, Miriam Stern, to design the letters (she, too, is acknowledged on the lining). She did this for Ethan's tallit as well, two years later. When designing a tallit for my sons, I felt I was restricted to fewer colors and nothing too lustrous. But the huge letters flowing across the back made a bold statement in and of themselves.

Three years later I found myself making a tallit for my daughter Elizabeth's Bat Mitzvah. Her parashah was *Shelakh Lekha*, and it includes the grapes, pomegranates, and figs that spies brought back from the Promised Land. Now I could embroider and bead to my heart's content, embellish every fruit, and even paint her verses. By then I had taken silk painting courses and so her atarah was painted a dark purple to contrast with the light purple of the tallit. The letters were outlined in a silver resist and filled with a lighter shade of purple.

The last tallit I made in this style was for my sister's fiftieth birthday.

When my daughter Elizabeth got married, she wanted a very simple tallit for her wedding: white embroidery on white fabric with small pearls on the letters.

Not everyone in my family has clamored for a handmade tallit. My husband has stayed with his traditional tallitot—only asking me to repair them from time to time. Indeed, I should add that only my sister wears the tallit I made for her on a daily basis. My sons prefer a traditional black-striped tallit for everyday worship. Ironically, since my tallitot are museum-quality, they are worn only for special occasions. For daily use, I myself don other less ornamented ones that I have made.

Over the years I have been approached by people to make them tallitot, but two factors mitigated against it: (1) the amount I would have to charge for my labor and (2) I cannot bear to part with my creations. Nor did I want to do cookie-cutter repetitions. Instead, I decided to give workshops in making tallitot. These are open to people at all levels of sewing expertise. For even a basic running stitch, when used with yarns of varying colors and textures, can produce a most complex design when appliquéing. Or you can buy a beautiful piece of fabric, create an atarah, and attach tzitzit. I wrote a curriculum and have gotten much pleasure in passing on my skills, helping women mostly—but some men, too—find their creative voice and enhance their spiritual lives.

**Menorah Rotenberg** is a psychotherapist practicing in Teaneck, New Jersey. She is a fabric artist and writer as well. Her article, "A Portrait of Rebecca," was published in *Conservative Judaism* in Spring 2002, and her Dvar Torah on *Vayeshev*, "A Hidden Master Plot," appeared in the *Forward* in December 2003.

# Finding My Way

*Cantor Geri Zeller*

I grew up in a modern Orthodox shul where women were not allowed on the bimah. Nor did women wear tallitot or kippot. My spiritual journey brought me through the Conservative movement and, eventually, into the Reform movement. I have been the cantor of my congregation in Pearl River, New York, for eighteen years now.

During the second year at my synagogue, I decided to make my own tallit over the summer. As a woman, I was exempt from the commandment to wear a fringed garment. I had chosen to do so and I wanted that tallit to reflect what that decision meant to me.

I had a vague idea that the part of the tallit across my back would be a tree of life, an *etz hayim*, reflecting talmudic scholars' view that the Torah itself is a tree of life. And I discovered, as artist friends had told me, that in creating a work of art, the piece takes on a life of its own. This was certainly true of my tallit, as I began searching through fabric stores for material that would bring my vision to life.

First, I found wide-wale brown corduroy for the trunk of the tree. Next I came across a black lace that I used to form a Torah growing out of the tree trunk. Then I happened upon a golden-scaled fabric that became the tablets of the commandments, the golden core of the Torah.

From behind the leaves of the tree emerge beams of light, because the Torah adds light to our lives. The corners of my tallit have flowers, because the teachings of the Torah flower in our minds. I was fortunate to find a *techelet* (blue thread) kit from Israel, so the tzitzit have the required blue thread. And the tree is set against a sky-blue background.

For the atarah, the band across the neck that usually bears the words of the blessing the men say when they put on a tallit, I again chose something especially meaningful for me. Since women wear a tallit by choice rather than obligation, my atarah bears the words of the *Birkat Kohanim*, the Priestly Benediction, because my father was a kohein. The tree is done as a three-dimensional soft sculpture, which makes the tallit weighty, so that I am very conscious that I am wearing a fringed garment during prayer.

Every time I drape my specially made tallit around my shoulders, I feel wrapped in God's love. This tallit, which reflects my rootedness in Judaism and in life, makes me feel wholly (and holy) connected to God, to the Jewish people, and to my own deepest spirit.

Cantor Geri Zeller, a wife, mother, and Bubbe, lives in Hillsdale, New Jersey. The Cantor for eighteen years at Beth Am Temple, in Pearl River, New York, she is soon to be named Cantor Emeritus.

# These Are the Fringes That Bind Us Together

### Susan North Gilboa

*[Editor's Note: This is the text of a talk given when the author's daughter was presented with a tallit upon becoming a bat mitzvah on December 16, 2001.]*

I had been to workshops where we were asked to create a tallit—a family tallit, or a tallit that expresses something about us. Then, the year before I turned forty, I decided that it was time for me to wrap myself in my own tallit. To feel the warmth and sense of embrace that I felt when my father wrapped his tallit around me. To collect the memories while holding the fringes that bind us together from generation to generation.

I mentioned this to my husband Rami and he said, "OK, if you think it's a good idea, get one." Get one? He was being supportive, but I knew that I didn't want to just "get one," so the idea remained just that—an idea. I turned forty and still didn't have a tallit of my own. The month after my fortieth birthday, I went to the Hanukkah Fair at Valley Beth Shalom in Los Angeles where I met Smadar, an artist who paints on silk. Besides making beautiful scarves, she also paints tallitot. I knew that this kind of hand-painted tallit was what I wanted, but on that day I just took her business card.

The following month, January, I flew to New York for my Oma Jenny's funeral. During the shiva my mom gave me a beautiful lace tablecloth that my Oma had always used on Shabbat. It was at that moment that I knew I was beginning the journey of creating my tallit. Three months later, I wrapped myself in a colorful painted tallit with free-form dancers, vibrant roses, and musical notes. The inside lining was a piece of my Oma's Shabbat tablecloth.

There wasn't a doubt in my mind that part of this tablecloth should also be part of [my daughter] Talia's tallit when she became a bat mitzvah, especially because of the special relationship that she had with my Oma. Talia helped Smadar design her tallit with musical notes, beautiful butterflies, and sunflower buds emerging into sunflowers. She chose to complete the tallit with the lace from my Oma's Shabbat tablecloth as the fringes on both ends.

While on my journey through this process, I also became interested in "crazy quilt" and "keeping quilt" ideas. So, in addition to the lace from my Oma on our tallitot, I wanted to incorporate in Talia's tallit symbols of people from far away yet close to our hearts. I wanted to create something on a piece of material that connects them—and people once dear to her but no longer with us—to Talia. Talia's tallit bag and the matching quilt/wall hanging were created by family and friends far and near who are pieces of the fabric of Talia's life.

What a special journey it has been for me from the moment it began. Continuing the journey with Talia made it much more spiritually meaningful than I had ever imagined or dreamed it could be. I want to thank everyone who took the time to fashion a unique contribution, and I want to thank Talia for sharing the journey with me.

Together we want to thank my Mom, Talia's Grandma Bunny (North), for helping to spark the idea for these distinctive tallitot by giving me her mother's tablecloth and for giving Talia the gift of her tallit in honor of becoming a bat mitzvah.

*(The same Shabbat tablecloth was made into a shawl, as noted below. What follows was a short speech given by the author at her mother Bunny's seventy-fifth birthday party.)*

AS WE COME together to celebrate you and this special milestone in your life, the journey has come full circle. As your daughter, I feel blessed to be sharing life's journey with you, and then to have you as an integral part of Rami's, Talia's, and Aviv's lives is a triple blessing.

Today we have something we want to present to you so that you can also share the fabric of our lives as it weaves together our wonderful legacy of faith, love, and tradition. It connects us to generations past and those yet to come.

Don't worry: We haven't made you a tallit, although the thought did cross my mind. Instead, we made a shawl for you with a piece of Oma's Shabbat tablecloth, and in each corner there is part of a napkin that she used to embroider on. One corner has her initials, which she embroidered herself; another corner has your initials; *Mazal Tov* appears on another corner; and our names adorn the fourth.

May you wear it in good health and in happiness. And should you ever choose to make a tallit out of it, it's easy to do.

**Susan North Gilboa**, a native of Flushing (Queens), New York, and her husband Rami, born and raised in Israel, have two children, a daughter, Talia, and a son, Aviv. Residents of Encino, California, the family belongs to Valley Beth Shalom Synagogue, a Conservative synagogue in Encino. Ms. Gilboa, a Jewish educator and coordinator of the nationally known Shaare Tikva and Moreshet special education programs, was also one of the founders of the B'Yachad youth program for children with special needs. In addition, she has been an Israeli folk dance instructor for hundreds of children and adults in New York and Los Angeles.

# A Tallit's Purpose
# Becomes Clear

*Hannah Sue Margolis*

My dad came to this country as a very young boy. His father and a large group of fellow Lithuanians decided to go to South Africa and strike it rich in the fabled gold mines at the tip of the African continent. Fortunately, his mom decided to move to New York. So my dad and his three brothers and one sister settled in Brooklyn with their mother. About twelve years later his dad showed up in Brooklyn with barely a penny to his name.

Dad worked as a glasscutter most of his adult life, after serving in the Army in World War I. The highlight of his career was installing the glass that separated the translators from the members of the United Nations at the UN headquarters in Manhattan.

Like many of us living in Brooklyn, we knew we were Jewish and celebrated the holidays. Although Mom and Dad were raised in Orthodox homes, neither my brother nor I went to services. They didn't give us any formal Jewish education. My brother did have a Bar Mitzvah to make our grandparents happy. He learned the prayers by memorizing them from a phonograph record.

My adult life was spent as a physical therapist in the U.S. Air Force. This career sent me all over the world. I soon realized that I didn't like going to Happy Hour on Friday evening. My best excuse to get out of drinking was to go to Shabbat services. Shortly after I began going to services, I found myself drawn to the Shabbat ritual: It was no longer an excuse I made to get out of Happy Hour, but a deeply felt desire to connect with my Jewish roots.

I didn't start weaving until after I retired from the military. I was volunteering at the Institute of Texan Cultures, and instructors there showed me how to demonstrate the art of weaving. I decided I needed to learn more, so I enrolled in professional classes.

A Catholic friend (a nun) mentioned that a "prayer shawl" was the best way she knew to block off the outside world when she wanted to pray. This gave me an idea: Weaving tallitot would add a spiritual dimension to my weaving life, incorporating my love of Judaism and my passion for weaving. I also wanted to create something that no other weaver in San Antonio was even considering. At that point I didn't know what I would do with my very first tallit; I just knew I wouldn't sell it.

When Dad was in his early nineties, Mom and Dad moved into a senior citizens' apartment house run by a Jewish agency in Brooklyn. With the help of a visiting rabbi, Dad tried saying a few prayers on special holidays. By now I was quite comfortable with my Judaism, and was most pleased to see Dad returning to his.

When Dad died at ninety-five, I knew he wanted to be laid to rest wearing a tallit, as is customary. At that point I realized what I had been saving this very first tallit for. I still get tears in my eyes whenever I tell this story.

To date I have woven more than fifty tallitot for both adults and children about to become b'nai mitzvah. One congregation actually ordered a tallit for their rabbi's first service. The rabbi herself designed the neckband, fashioned in cross-stitch, and requested that lavender roses be stitched on both ends to signify the love of growing roses that she and her husband shared.

Despite my passion for weaving tallitot, I myself do not wear a tallit. I have never felt comfortable wearing one, but I do derive a special joy from watching others wearing the tallitot that I have woven. My biggest thrill comes from watching someone don a tallit for the first time in front of a congregation.

**Hannah Sue Margolis**, who was born in Brooklyn, now lives in San Antonio. She spent twenty-seven years as a physical therapist in the Air Force, serving all over the world, including 2½ years in the early 1960s in Tripoli, Libya, where she volunteered in an Arab polio clinic. Now she volunteers with United Way, the Institute of Texan Cultures, and the Jewish Community Center, as well as teaching weaving at the Southwest School of Art and Craft.

# The Picture-Perfect Tallit

*Toby Gang*

This tale of the tallit is a mix of pain and comfort, and ultimately a family's blessing. It began in the summer of 2003, six months before my son Alex's Bar Mitzvah, and six months after my mother began a year-long series of infections and surgeries that precluded her from living independently in an apartment. As we pored through my mother's belongings so she could move permanently into a nursing home, we came upon my late father's tallit. I offered it to my brother, but also said that my son would probably like to wear it for his Bar Mitzvah in January, since he was sad that his grandfather was gone. My sister-in-law Ellen, who is talented and creative, remarked, "I bet I could put your father's Bar Mitzvah picture on the tallit."

So began the journey to what became the highlight of Alex's Bar Mitzvah—his custom-made, picture-perfect tallit.

As summer turned to fall and the Bar Mitzvah approached, it became apparent that my mother would not live to see Alex's Bar Mitzvah. And so, as Ellen began to design the tallit, she thought she might incorporate a picture of my mother as well as my father. And then she added wedding pictures of both sets of Alex's grandparents, as well as a wedding photo of his parents.

The tallit that evolved is a photograph album of Alex's family history—all the people who have loved him, who were present at his Bar Mitzvah, or who were there in spirit. Each side of the tallit contains the story of those who preceded him—the late 1920s Bar Mitzvah photos of his grandfathers (short pants and all), weddings, Alex with his grandfather, Alex with his older brother, his parents as children with their siblings, and, of course, his father as a Bar Mitzvah.

Ellen presented Alex with his grandfather's tallit as a surprise gift the evening before the Bar Mitzvah. And on that special Saturday morning, Alex knew that he was truly draped in the love of his family. As he recited his prayers and Torah portion, and received the blessings of his family and community, Alex was seen to grasp the photos of his missing grandparents, wrap them more closely around him, and even bring them to his lips.

As the tallit eloquently told the story of our family, there wasn't a dry eye in the synagogue.

**Toby Gang** lives in Wynnewood, Pennsylvania, with her husband, Joel Hirsh, and sons Robert and Alex. She is a Business Manager for AT&T, and is a member of the Board of Trustees of Beth David Reform Congregation in Gladwyne, Pennsylvania.

# Rediscovering a Tallit

*Deborah Lurie Edery*

My husband, Yaacov Edery, received his tallit in the moshav Sde David near Ashkelon, Israel, in a group B'nai Mitzvah celebration in 1956. His father gave him this tallit, a simple blue and white child's tallit, with beautiful golden embroidery on the atarah. Yaacov's grandfather had been the chief rabbi in Casablanca, Morocco, and the family had made aliyah (immigrated to Israel) in the early 1950s from Morocco.

The last time we visited Israel I decided that my husband needed a "manly" tallit. So my sister-in-law and I went shopping in Tel Aviv and I surprised him with a new tallit.

When our daughter, Jessica Tali Edery, was about to become bat mitzvah, we searched for the perfect tallit. There were so many attractive tallitot in stores and online. My daughter and I both agreed that a tallit was not a fashion statement, yet all the tallitot we saw seemed so trendy. We wanted to find one that she would treasure always and not outgrow. Her Bat Mitzvah was approaching, and I was getting concerned. Would we find one in time?

One Shabbat I was sitting next to my husband in synagogue and suddenly realized that we already had the perfect tallit! We went to the craft and sewing store with the tallit that my husband had received forty-five years before and headed for the ribbon aisle. We sat on the floor, placing various ribbons against the tallit, trying to find the perfect match that would transform it into a woman's tallit.

Suddenly, we looked up and discovered two older women, a mother and daughter perhaps, staring down at us. I said, "I'll bet you're wondering what we are doing."

"No," one of the women answered. "You are decorating a tallit for your daughter. How nice!"

We chose a beautiful ribbon with a floral pattern embroidered in blue, white, and silver, which matched the tallit. It was just enough to transform the tallit into a tallit all her own. I bought a tallit bag that matched and added the ribbon accent to complete the set.

My husband proudly handed our daughter her tallit when she became bat mitzvah.

While many of the girls in her class have filed their tallitot away in a drawer, Jessica wears hers every time we go to services, and she is proud to have such a distinctive tallit, imbued with family history, personalized accents, and her mother's love sewn into the very fabric of the fringed shawl she calls her own.

**Deborah Lurie Edery** is the Activity Director/Service Coordinator for an assisted living community, Laurel Gardens of Woodbridge, Connecticut. She team teaches third-grade Hebrew school (with her husband and daughter) at B'Nai Israel Religious School in Southbury, Connecticut, and lives in Hamden, Connecticut. She is also a polymer clay artisan, concentrating mostly on Judaica.

# Allison's Bat Mitzvah Tallit

*Helene Goodman*

B ack in 1999, my sister Jill called to tell me that a date had been set for her daughter Allison's Bat Mitzvah; it was September 15, 2001. At the time, I didn't even have a 2001 calendar! I wrote the date on a hot pink Post-it note, and stuck it on my corkboard.

Shortly after the date was set, Jill asked me if I would make Allison's tallit. I accepted the challenge, and soon the tallit became a project. It began with a needlepoint collar (28 x 3 inches) that would ultimately be attached to a ready-made tallit (or so I thought). The big joke in the family became "Will Helene finish it in time for the Bat Mitzvah?"

I worked on the needlepoint on and off for close to a year. When the needlepoint was completed, I started searching for a tallit that was the right size, but nothing seemed quite right. At the suggestion of the woman who oversees the gift shop at a local temple, I decided to make the tallit myself. I had no idea what I was about to undertake! I visited the local fabric shop and found some lovely white fabric, and set it aside.

It was now early August 2001—plenty of time to complete the project. I cut the fabric to dimensions that would fit Allison (60 x 18 inches). I hand-stitched the hem on all four sides, and stitched the collar to one edge. This alone took an entire day. I took one look at the expanse of white fabric with its needlepoint collar on one edge and thought to myself, "Oh my God! This looks awful." It was just so stark. I thought that a design on each corner might do the trick. I dug out a book of needlepoint and cross-stitch designs and found one that was simple and would complement the collar.

I headed off to the needlepoint shop and, after some trial and error, found the right materials. Over the Labor Day weekend, I embroidered the corners, each of which took six hours. The results were looking good! The tallit wasn't going anywhere if I didn't like it. I finally finished it and took it to the cleaners on September 5—plenty of time! I wasn't going to be sewing my way cross-country to the site of Allison's Bat Mitzvah. My flight from California to New Jersey (via Atlanta) was scheduled for September 12.

The final step was adding the tzitzit. I had ordered the loose cords from a tallit company in New York, and they arrived on September 10. (OK—this was close.) It took me a while to realize that the strands were not the correct length—they were all the same, which made it impossible to knot them according to the strict guidelines. Plan B was implemented: I used the same Perle cotton that I had used for the needlepoint and embroidery. I got the hang of tying them and had the four corners finished on September 11.

The tallit looked great and I was really pleased with the results. I was pretty sure that Allison would love it. Regardless, I had reached the point of no return.

I had begun packing on September 10, using Big Red (a twenty-six-inch piece of expandable luggage, capable of holding three weeks' worth of clothing!). Everything was in Big Red, and the tallit was in a ziplock bag in my carry-on bag.

On Tuesday morning, September 11, I was awake before sunrise. It was around 5 a.m. on the West Coast, and since I had to get up even earlier for my flight the next day, I decided to begin the day as I always do: I headed downstairs to make coffee and catch up with the local news station.

Around 5:50 PST, the local news team said that there was a breaking story—a fire in the World Trade Center in Lower Manhattan. The station switched to *Good Morning America* with a live shot of the Twin Towers. I could see smoke, but also noticed that part of the building appeared to be missing. A moment later, Peter Jennings appeared, and no more than five minutes passed before all of us saw the second plane deliberately smash into the second tower. It was a stunning sight, which left most of us speechless.

My first thought was, "I hope my family is not watching this." That was a short-lived thought as the phone rang later that morning. My second thought was, "I have Allison's tallit." For a while, I didn't realize what the impact would be on the country. Then I heard that all air traffic had been halted. I watched the news until it became too painful to watch.

Later that day, I called Delta Airlines and spoke to a reservations agent. First, I rescheduled my flight for Thursday, September 13, then Friday, September 14. There was a ritual going on: Call Delta, call home, and call the shuttle service. And after each call, I had the same thought: I have Allison's tallit.

These were difficult days. With each call to Mom, I could hear the heaviness in her voice. Friends and acquaintances tried to talk me out of making the trip. It never even crossed my mind. If the FAA gave the airports and airlines clearance to fly, then I was going to be on a plane.

I arrived at the bustling airport at 6:30 on Friday morning for an 8:45 flight. When I finally got to the counter, I learned that my flight was going to be delayed a couple of hours due to mechanical problems. Security was fairly heavy, but no one seemed to mind.

Once we got past security, most of us headed to Applebee's for some breakfast. After checking the timetables, I learned that my flight was delayed again— this time until 1:00. The flight was delayed yet again, and around 3:00 we began the boarding process. Everyone was very orderly and as we got settled into our seats, we had no idea that this plane was not going to be leaving Ontario, California.

Once everyone was seated, we taxied out onto the runway. It was a full flight. After a few moments, we heard the pilot tell us that there was yet another problem. So we headed back to the gate and stayed seated while the mechanics checked the plane. After twenty or thirty minutes, we were told that the plane needed some more work. I was sitting toward the rear, and by the time I got out of the plane, there were very long lines at the gates.

One of the ticket agents told us that another flight was heading for Atlanta (my connecting city) and that there were fifty seats available on that flight. Our options were to wait and see if the first plane could be repaired, or reschedule our flight. My first thought was, "If I can get to Atlanta tonight, I can fly to Newark on Saturday morning." It will be close, but I may be able to get there in time for the service. I started to think about how I could get a seat on that flight. I had Allison's tallit.

There were at least fifteen people ahead of me. I pulled out $50 from my handbag, took a deep breath, and walked straight to the front of the line. I said to the man, "You're going to think this is absolutely crazy, but I am desperate to get to Newark. My niece is having her Bat Mitzvah in the morning and the service begins at 10:00. I need to get on this flight to Atlanta. If you would allow me to step in front of you, I will give you $50."

He looked at me and quietly said, "Please—You are more than welcome to stand in line in front of me, but I cannot take your money. If I took your money, I would not feel good about this." I thanked him profusely, and we headed to the ticket counter simultaneously.

As I started to explain my predicament to the ticket agent, I learned that the flight was already full. I would not be on that flight to Atlanta. I then found out that there was a flight at 10:45 that evening from LAX. Delta provided me with a travel voucher and told me where to pick up my luggage. I retrieved Big Red, and got on the shuttle that would take me to LAX.

After a harrowing ride from one airport to the next, we finally arrived at LAX at 6:00 p.m. I was going to be flying from L.A. to Cincinnati, then on to Newark. Newark Airport had been shut down for part of the day, but was now open. I took this as a good sign.

I still had four hours to go. I wasn't very hungry, so I set my sights on some ice cream. I was doing my best to keep everyone in New Jersey (family and shuttle service) informed of my progress. By this time, I had missed the Friday evening service. I was still hopeful that I would arrive by Saturday morning. I had a very heavy heart. Allison's tallit never left my side.

It was a long evening, indeed, but it was finally time to head to the gate. The inbound aircraft arrived a little later than planned. It was a Boeing 767—a huge plane that can carry well over 250 people. It took quite some time for the passengers to disembark. Then the plane had to be cleaned. It was already past 11:00, and by the time we were all on board, it was way past the 10:45 departure time. As we listened to the pilot, we heard that the flight was scheduled to arrive in Cincinnati around 7:15 in the morning. This was not good news: My departure time for Newark was precisely 7:15 a.m.

We arrived in Cincinnati right at 7:15, and the other passengers and I began to file out. I was horrified to learn that the 7:15 to Newark had departed without me. I found the nearest gate agent, and learned that I had been rebooked on the 10:50 flight to Newark. I took my new boarding pass and headed toward the ladies' room. I went into one of the stalls and cried.

After I composed myself and had a quick breakfast, I did some walking: It was better than sitting for what would be another three hours. Finally, the clock approached 10:00 a.m. Time to get fixed up a bit. I brushed my teeth, washed my face, put in my contact lenses, and added some makeup. I looked like hell—I had not slept well, and I looked it.

I went back to the boarding area, and waited to take my seat on board. And waited and waited. Finally, we were in our seats (not an empty seat on the plane, mind you), and we were not moving. As I looked out the window, I saw luggage coming off the ramp. I thought that was odd. Then I saw Big Red! This was really peculiar.

After a few moments, the pilot made the following announcement: "Ladies and gentlemen, thank you for your patience. There were a couple of passengers who did not like their seat assignments and were giving us a hard time about it. In light of the recent events, we thought it best to remove them from the flight. We are in the process of retrieving their luggage. As far as I'm concerned, they can take a bus to Newark. We will be departing shortly and thank you for putting your trust in us to get you safely to your destination."

We were under way at 11:30. As we approached Newark, the New York City skyline became visible. On final approach, those of us on the right side of the plane could see downtown New York. Smoke was still rising from the area where the majestic Twin Towers had once proudly stood. We will never forget that sight.

WELL, THE TALLIT and I had made it to Newark. The next hurdle was to find the shuttle driver from Olympic Limousine. I headed to the baggage claim area, and realized that I could not remember the name of the limo service! Finally, the name Olympic popped into my head, but I still did not see a driver holding a card with my name on it. Please, not today, I thought. It was already 1:30 in the afternoon. The service was over, but the party would be going on till 4 or 5: We needed to get going.

After a moment or two, I found him. His name was Bob. "I could kiss you," I said.

"Why?" he asked.

"Because my niece had her Bat Mitzvah this morning. We're going to a party. By the way, Bob, I need to change into my party clothes and I'll be doing it the car." I asked him to put Big Red on the back seat next to me, and I slid in and opened the bag.

First things first, I thought to myself. Off with the Reeboks and jeans. Socks next. After a struggle, I managed to get my pantyhose on; shoes next, followed by my skirt. The skirt was a cinch because it was a wrap skirt—just had to scoot it under my butt and I was good to go. I disconnected my insulin pump, so I wouldn't get it tangled in the tubing, and reconnected it once the skirt was buttoned.

Shirt next. I pulled off my T-shirt (yes, I was wearing a bra) and pulled on the fancy one. It was a sleeveless tank, which was pretty narrow. I got my first arm through, and could feel my bra getting twisted around behind my back. Oy! It took several minutes before I was able to declare success. With the exception of my cardigan, I was completely dressed! Not bad. And there was time to spare.

Bob and I conversed throughout this quick-change operation, and I found out that he was a stockbroker who had worked for a company that had been downsizing. He was married and had three children. He told me that he had recently interviewed with an investment company that was located in the World Trade Center. God works in mysterious ways.

He had a calming effect on me, and I was totally relaxed by the time we got to the reception. When I got out of his car, he tucked in the label that was sticking out from my sweater, and sent me into the reception with good wishes.

Once inside the reception, I saw a sea of familiar faces and bodies. I turned over the tallit to my sister Jill and she went to find Allison. Mission (finally!) accomplished.

I DECIDED TO write this story for a few reasons, mostly as a way to exorcise the pain of having missed Allison's Bat Mitzvah. Weeks later, I still could not believe that I was unable to be there. I know in my head that I had done everything possible to be there, but my heart was broken, nonetheless. And through it all, I could not forget that thousands of lives were lost on 9/11. I don't ever want to lose sight of that, as sad as I am about my personal story.

My nephew Adam is now seven, and we have six years to go until his Bar Mitzvah. I won't miss that one, and I should probably get started on his tallit ...

**Helene Goodman** was born in Paterson, New Jersey, moved to California in 1986, and returned to New Jersey in 2002. She now lives in Toms River, New Jersey. Working in sales and customer service most of her professional life, Ms. Goodman is the Northeast Regional Manager for Agent Sales for FleetHawk, an automatic vehicle location device.

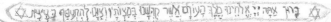

# SAVED FROM THE ASHES: HOLOCAUST-ERA TALLITOT

The sheer horror of the Holocaust, the genocide of six million, defies description and even explanation. The only way we seem to be able to come to grips with this twentieth-century nightmare is by telling stories.

In the poem and essays that follow, writers focus on various aspects of the Holocaust and World War II, and how tallitot—their own, their relatives', one of unknown provenance, one on display in a museum case—managed to survive the war years. These stories recall this tumultuous era from the fringes, and give voice to voices long silenced.

Like the Jewish practice of placing a pebble on a tombstone, these essays honor people who have passed on, many in unimaginable circumstances. Yet hope, too, emerges from these pages, as we see Judaism and Jewish life still thriving in the shadow of this, the darkest period in our history. And we vow never to forget.

—Diana Drew

# Tallitot at Auschwitz

*Davi Walders*

That cold September, the wind blew
off the steppes across Oswiecim,
but could not touch the thousands
of tallitot filling glass museum cases.

Black and blue stripes on white graying
like ash hung from crossbars; their tzitzit
lay in dust on the floor. Row after row
like guards, so many, unkissed, unworn,

just hanging in a silent room. The case reads
"Jewish fringed garments." I ask the guard
if they could be raised so the tzitzit wouldn't
drag in the dust. He shrugs. I ask the guide.

She shrugs. I write a letter to the director,
hear nothing. They are still there in those
musty cases, dangling above cell block 11.
No one can redeem them, those silent threads
shredding in the dust of what happened there.

**Davi Walders** is a poet, writer, and educator, who lives in Chevy Chase, Maryland. Her poetry and prose have been published in more than 150 anthologies and other publications, including the *American Scholar*, *Ms.*, and *JAMA*. She developed and directs the Vital Signs Poetry Project at the National Institutes for Health, and received Hadassah of Greater Washington's 2002 Myrtle Wreath Award for this work.

# A Tallit Rescued from the Ashes

## Estelle Sofer

W orld War II had just come to a close, and Sam Gertel, of blessed memory, had miraculously survived the daily brutalities of the Majdanek Concentration Camp. As the camp was being liberated, Sam found and kept two precious things: a little girl named Feigele, shivering and covered with lice, and a tallit, both of which had also survived the horrors of the Holocaust.

Sam had grown up in Poland, where he was captured by the Nazis and sent to the concentration camp. His first wife and son had been killed by the Nazis, and Feigele, the little girl, had lost her parents in the Holocaust as well. Sam, whose heart went out to Feigele, took in the child and raised her as his own, nursing her back to health. Subsequently, he married a lovely woman named Mathilda, who loved Feigele too. Sam and Mathilda wanted to adopt the little girl, but never did. Perhaps Feigele was always hoping to locate and reclaim her own family.

But Sam and his wife took care of her, loved her, and gave her a good home. Feigele is now in her sixties and living on a kibbutz in Israel with her own family.

Meanwhile, Sam moved to the United States, bringing with him the precious tallit, whose original owner he never knew. He and Mathilda settled in Hollis Hills, Queens, and had two daughters of their own—Yola and Barbara. Sam worked hard as a building contractor and became well-to-do. His *tzedakah* (philanthropic generosity) was renowned in the community.

The tallit Sam rescued from the ashes, a traditional blue and white prayer shawl, is now in tatters. It can't even be washed, because it would fall apart. Yet it has a place of honor in the Duchan Gallery of the Hollis Hills Jewish Center, covering some rare books. Sam decided to donate the tallit to the gallery, one of the first Judaica art museums established in a synagogue, so others could see and reflect on this treasured remnant—this other survivor of the Holocaust.

**Estelle Sofer** is the founder and curator of the Duchan Gallery at the Hollis Hills (NY) Jewish Center. She is also a former Sisterhood president. Her husband's family is believed to be descended from the Chatam Sofer of Czechoslovakia, a renowned rabbi. She was a neighbor of Sam Gertel, of blessed memory.

# The Special Tallit

### Rabbi Yisrael Gordon

Spring 1946. World War II had ended less than a year before. The thousands of Polish Jews who had fled to Russia at the outbreak of the war were finally allowed to return home. This forced relocation of Polish Jews was actually a case of a curse turning into a blessing, because most of these Polish Jews had settled in Asiatic Russia, in towns like Tashkent, Kastrama, and Samarkand, where the war and the deprivation hadn't reached

Native Russian Jews, meanwhile, saw this new development as a God-given opportunity to escape the country whose communist leaders had made their lives miserable for close to thirty years. These Russian Jews had maintained their Judaism and their Jewish traditions, lived a Torah life, built shuls, schools, and mikvaot secretly—all at risk of their lives. Hundreds died in Siberian gulags. Yet, encouraged and guided by their leader, the Lubavitcher rebbe, thousands survived despite all the abuse they had endured at the hands of their non-Jewish compatriots.

As if by divine revelation, the Jews in Russia had a brainstorm. Many Polish Jews had died during the war years, and their deaths had never been recorded. So Russian Jews simply adopted their identities and left Russia—illegally, of course—en masse.

Among the organizers and leaders of this surreptitious mass exodus was Reb Mendel Futerfas, a scion of a prominent Lubavitcher family and a former student at the yeshiva in the town of Lubavitch. But when he tried

to leave Russia himself (the rest of his family had emi-
grated several months earlier), Reb Mendel was caught,
convicted, and sentenced to ten years in a Siberian
prison. While the former yeshiva student was serving
his sentence, his tallit was torn to shreds. Unable to
replace it, Reb Mendel made himself a tallit out of burlap
bags, affixing homespun woolen tzitzit to its four corners. When he was finally released from prison, he was
forbidden to leave Russia. In the mid-1960s, however, he
did manage to leave, in pain physically but stronger
than ever spiritually and emotionally.

Reb Mendel first went to Israel, to visit the holy
places in Jerusalem, Sefad, Hebron, Meron, and throughout the country. The tallit he wore for his prayers was the
same burlap prayer shawl he had fashioned in Russia.

Rabbi Ephraim Wolff, director of the Lubavitcher
yeshivot in Kfar Chabad and Lod, saw Reb Mendel's
tallit and immediately took action, ordering a tallit
*mehuderet*, one of first-quality wool, handspun, and of a
large enough size (in both width and length) to satisfy all
the halachic requirements (those mandated by strict
Jewish law). When informed that there was sufficient
new wool for two more tallitot, Rabbi Wolff agreed to
have them made as well. They were beautiful and
kosher according to the strictest standards.

Reb Mendel was presented with the first tallit. The
second was sent to my father in Brooklyn, Reb Yochanan
Gordon, a devoted friend of Reb Mendel's family. The
third one Rabbi Wolff kept for himself.

My father, Reb Yochanan, wore this tallit proudly for
many years on Shabbat and the High Holy Days in the
Lubavitcher rebbe's synagogue, where he was the *gabbai*
(the one who calls people to the Torah).

In August 1969, I came to Brooklyn from Worcester,
Massachusetts, where I was living, to attend a Hasidic
gathering honoring the Lubavitcher rebbe's father's
*yahrzeit*. I went to see my father and he asked me to
attach (by winding and knotting in the prescribed way)
a new set of tzitzit to his special tallit.

I responded, "Father, I am here only for a few hours.
I don't have the time or patience to do this properly."

My father's humble response was this: "My dear son, how many times have I asked for a favor from you, Heaven knows, in how many years? Please . . ."

I ran to the store that sells religious articles, purchased the tzitzit, and attached them properly, befitting the expert my father thought (pardon the boast) I was. My father was pleased, and we exchanged hugs, a seventy-five-year-old father and a thirty-nine-year-old son.

Nine days later my father passed away suddenly. After the shiva, his four children each took certain of his religious items. I chose this tallit. He was laid to rest in another, older tallit.

For several years I prayed in this special tallit daily. When the wear began to show, I began using this tallit only on Shabbat and Holy Days and the day of his *yahrzeit*, the twenty-ninth of Av.

When I put on this tallit and see my reflection caught in the glass doors of the shul bookcase, I see my father, whom I resemble so much, and it is as if he were there by my side.

**Rabbi Yisrael Gordon** serves as Director of Administration at the Rabbinical College of America in Morristown, New Jersey. For twenty-eight years, he was principal of Hebrew studies at the Lubavitch Yeshiva in Worcester, Massachusetts.

# Life's Hidden Messages

## Marshall Botkin

I spent a good part of one recent spring traveling in Russia and Siberia as part of a sabbatical from my college. That summer, I decided to take my wife Sharon with me so she could meet my Russian friends and perhaps come to know and love the country and its people as I do. Before leaving, I went through the packing ritual that we all practice in preparation for trips to faraway places. One of the last items to go into the suitcase was the bag containing my tallit and tefillin. It was my plan to take advantage of all opportunities to perform my daily prayer ritual. Next to my bag was another bag containing a large tallit that had belonged to my uncle. As I packed the first bag, I heard a voice tell me distinctly, "Pack your uncle's tallit. Someone needs it."

Some years before, my uncle, Phil Soroka, had passed away. My uncle was very proud of his Jewish heritage and of being a patriotic American. He spoke and understood Yiddish, attended shul as often as possible, and fought with General George S. Patton against the Nazi terror in World War II. During his last few years, my uncle would sit in the sanctuary at the Children of Israel synagogue in Athens, Georgia. Draped in his massive tallit, he would tell the children stories from the history of the Jewish people and from his own life experiences. I know they liked "Uncle Phil," and I know he loved the children. When he died, his tallit was left to me. A great honor to be sure, but I already had two tallitot. So my uncle's tallit was rarely used except on the day of his *yahrzeit*, when I would say kaddish for him at my synagogue in Frederick, Maryland.

So I packed his tallit and left with my wife for our three-week adventure to Russia and Siberia. The first two weeks we spent in St. Petersburg and Western Siberia. However, on the fifteenth day of our trip, we found ourselves in Birobidzhan.

Birobidzhan is located in the Russian Far East, in an area known as the Jewish Autonomous Region. This sector of Siberia was set aside by Josef Stalin in 1928 in an attempt to resettle Jews all together and to force them to assimilate and embrace Marxist doctrine. Russian Jews were prompted to go to Siberia either by force or by the promise of a better life. They were unaware of the hidden assimilationist motive.

Of course, Stalin's plan did not work. To my mind, his scheme failed because any time Jewish people get together, they organize. The Jewish settlers in Siberia—many from the Ukraine and places like Kiev—set up a synagogue, Jewish schools, Jewish theater companies, and Jewish musical groups to play klezmer music. They spoke both Yiddish and Hebrew as well as Russian. In essence, they created a small, wholly Jewish region in the middle of Siberia.

Today, just outside of Birobidzhan, can be found the Yiddish Museum, which is housed in an old school building. Our museum guide, Marie, told us the story of these early Jewish settlers. She told us of the day when they received the first American tractor and how farm production increased as a result. She told us that during World War II the community sent 109 men—every able-bodied man in town—to fight the Nazis. For the Russian Jews living in the wilds of Siberia, fighting Nazis was paramount: Not only was there a Holocaust of the Jewish people (the 6 million), but there were 20 million Russians killed in the war as well. Like Uncle Phil, these early Jewish pioneers were proud of their Jewish heritage and considered themselves patriots (albeit to their native Russia).

In 1947, Stalin closed the Jewish theaters, the Jewish schools, and the synagogue, and forbade the speaking of Yiddish or Hebrew and the practice of any form of Judaism. He also burned all Yiddish- and Hebrew-language books as well as the holy books. This anti-Jewish edict remained in place until 1988 when, with the fall of the Soviet political system, new freedoms began to emerge. Thus, the story of the Jewish Autonomous Region now encompasses the last fourteen years, during which great strides have been made to recapture the region's lost heritage. The Yiddish Museum is an integral part of this process.

The purpose of the Yiddish Museum is to tell the story of these valiant Jewish settlers. It is also designed to relate to Jewish children the story of their religious heritage. Sharon and I were both very moved by the mission and the magnificent work being carried out by this institution, and felt we wanted to do something to promote the museum's goals. We asked Marie if we could make some kind of monetary contribution. She explained that they didn't need any money. What they desperately needed were Jewish ritual items to explain what the religion is all about. She had some yarmulkes and some makeshift menorahs. However, the number-one thing she needed was a tallit. She had asked the community center to give the museum one of these prayer shawls on several occasions, but such things are not easy to come by in Russia. A tallit exudes symbolism and speaks in its own way about the Jewish obligation to prayer. Finding one was next to impossible in the middle of Siberia.

Thus, at the moment of Marie's request, both Sharon and I were brought to tears. We had completely forgotten about packing my uncle's tallit, and the sudden realization of what had just happened was electrifying. We were moved spiritually, and once again we reaffirmed our belief that God works in mysterious ways.

So now Uncle Phil's tallit graces a display case in this wonderful Yiddish museum, in the middle of the Jewish Autonomous Region in Siberia. Each day it tells the story of the region's Jewish heritage to the many children who come through the doors. I know my uncle would have liked that.

**Marshall Botkin** is a Professor of Sociology at Frederick Community College in Frederick, Maryland. He has traveled extensively in the former Soviet Union, including Siberia, which is where Birobidzhan is located.

# The Adventurous Life of My Tallit

*Harry Arpadi*

My tallit made its appearance in time for my Bar Mitzvah, which took place in Berlin, Germany, in January 1937. It is a large, full-sized tallit, made from heavy wool with a collar woven with strong metallic yarn. Since we lived in the Jewish quarter of Berlin, I assume my mother bought it there. However, the tallit bag and a matching tefillin bag were lovingly hand-sewn by my aunt Golde, who had recently married my uncle Isaak, my mother's brother in Lithuania.

Tante Golde used heavy silk for these precious bags—green for the outside and white for the inside lining. With gold yarn she beautifully embroidered my initials, H. A., in Hebrew letters, and added a Star of David with the year—5697—inscribed inside.

Tante Golde was a beautiful woman, and I believe she was quite a bit younger than my uncle. No one would ever have imagined at the time that these exquisite bags she had made with such love and care would eventually become the only items to survive her and the only proof of her short-lived existence on earth—her only legacy. She, her husband, and her two little boys, my cousins, all perished on the first day of the Nazi invasion of Russia in June 1941. There were no Jewish survivors in the little town of Gargzdai, a town facing the German border, where they lived.

In January 1939 my tallit traveled with me and my

family from Berlin to Riga, Latvia, where we were permitted to live until we could obtain our immigration papers for the United States. In September 1940, my tallit, my parents, and I took the Siberian Express through Russia, Siberia, and Manchukuo, finally departing from Harbin by ship to Kobe, Japan, and then sailing from Yokohama to Seattle. From there we eventually crossed the United States, and I arrived in New York City at age sixteen. Two years later, at age eighteen, my tallit and I joined the U.S. Army.

Shipped overseas at the beginning of January 1943 as a combat engineer replacement, I landed in Naples, Italy. In my duffle bag, among all my GI clothing, were, of course, my tallit and tefillin, still in Tante Golde's beautiful green silk bags. Our group pitched pup tents in the vicinity of the bombed-out harbor, where we spent our first night on Italian soil. By morning, all our duffle bags were gone. Searching for them, we came across items the thieves apparently found useless and had abandoned. Among them: my tallit and tefillin inside their precious bags, along with a miniature prayer book, given to me by my parents.

Since then, I have rarely used that tallit. First of all, it is large and very warm, since it is made of wool. Additionally, the rough collar feels scratchy on my neck. However, I am delighted that it has been used at some of my children's weddings, lifted high on four poles by their siblings over the heads of the happy couple as a chuppah. And it has often been borrowed by friends for use as a chuppah as well.

I realize that I could choose to be buried in it, as is the custom, but I prefer to have my well-traveled tallit continue its journey as a loving legacy—as a chuppah for the weddings of my grandchildren and of the generations that follow. I hope this tradition will remind all my descendants of our family's past, as they remember those who are gone, while anticipating with joy the hopeful promise of the future.

**Harry Arpadi** was born in Berlin in 1924. He and his family left Germany in 1939, eventually arriving in New York in 1940 via the circuitous route described above. Now retired, Mr. Arpadi was President and Creative Director of an advertising agency that he founded. He and his wife, Adele (née Zang), who have been married for fifty-six years, live in Mount Vernon, New York, and are members of the Free Synagogue of Mount Vernon. They have four children and six grandchildren.

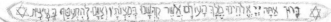

# THE HOLY LAND: TALLITOT FROM ISRAEL

Like one of G-d's biblical miracles, the State of Israel rose from the ashes of the Holocaust—a haven for Jews in a heartless world, the fulfillment of a biblical promise. Three years after the end of the darkest period in our history, the shining star of a permanent homeland glowed brightly, with the imprimatur of the United Nations and the support of the United States.

American Jews have always felt a special bond with Israel: We planted trees in Israel from our earliest days; we buy Israeli bonds; we visit the Holy Land; and some of us make aliyah (immigrate to Israel). The very notion of Israel, like the blue thread in the white tzitzit of a tallit, winds through our thinking, our consciousness, in often-unexpected ways. We may scan a newspaper, but stop to read the story with a dateline of Jerusalem. Whenever we hear about yet another suicide bombing in Israel, we say a prayer and our hearts go out to those who suffer in that sliver of a country that holds so much hope, so much love, so many of our deepest spiritual yearnings. We feel a dual citizenship, and do what we can to strengthen and encourage Jews living halfway around the world in the Promised Land.

The essays that follow capture glimpses of Israel through the threads of the tallit. One writer envisions the rectangular Israeli flag as a national tallit (minus the tzitzit). Another forges a quiet connection with a neighbor, who bequeaths her husband's tallit to him. In several others, we see how the fates of Jews in Israel and Jews in the United States are interwoven, just as the strands of the tallit intermingle to form a beautiful, unified whole.

Our relationship with Israel is at once complicated, nuanced, yet straightforward. Internal politics aside, Israel represents for all of us the fulfillment of our aspirations to nationhood, a homeland of our own, a state embodying Jewish values and Jewish sensibilities. Like the tallit itself, Israel offers us shelter and shalom (in its essential meaning—peace, integrity, wholeness) in a world fraught with tension and dissension.

—Diana Drew

# The Forty-Two-Year-Old Tallit
## Yitz (Ira) Rubin

In the summer of 1963 I went on one of the first Bar Mitzvah pilgrimages to Israel. About one hundred Bar/Bat Mitzvah–age youngsters were flown to Israel on El Al to experience the Holy Land firsthand, something most of their families had never done at that time. The group was under Conservative auspices and therefore followed the daily regimen of prayer and Shabbat observance.

We tasted the beauty of this still idealistic country by staying in villages set up for children making aliyah or in very rustic hotels. I do not remember ever seeing the names Hilton or Sheraton on our lodgings. Since the trip was early in the development of summers abroad, ours was a truly unique experience.

Each of the boys had come on the trip with the prerequisite tallit, presented at our Bar Mitzvah—no girls I knew had yet taken to wearing one. Each of these tallitot had a story. Whether they were given to us by parents, grandparents, or friends, they each had a signature warmth that enveloped us when used for Shabbat or other worship services. What we did not know, upon embarking on this trip, was that we were to be further blessed with a tallit from another, totally unexpected, source.

One day, we all piled into those old school buses with the hard seats, and headed to Jerusalem, to the home of Israel's president. It turned out that all of us were to have a visit with President Yitzchak Ben Zvi. At that time, none of us grasped what this meant—how rare it would be in our lifetimes to meet a head of state, much less the head of the Jewish state. Only much later did we realize the import of this remarkable invitation. Unfortunately, at the last moment President Ben Zvi was called away and could not meet with us himself, but Mrs. Ben Zvi apologized profusely and then spoke to us for a while in a large, very informal room. We were treated to *mitz tapusim* and *mitz eskoleyot*—the famous orange and grapefruit juices served on every street corner and kiosk in the country—along with some packaged cookies.

As the visit was coming to an end, each boy was given a tallit and everyone was also given a mezuzah. Immediately, all the boys began to use the new tallit—a gift from the president and the State of Israel. What a personal tie to this new country of ours! Carefully we packed away the tallit we had brought to Israel so we could use this new and awesome gift.

It is now forty-two years later and I have never replaced this tallit—the one I received from the State of Israel—despite its yellowing and slightly stained appearance. No matter when I use it, it brings back memories of a trip that changed my life in a myriad of ways.

I am tormented by conflicting needs—to keep this gift and not pack it away, and yet to purchase one that will wrap me securely in the world of tallitot more reminiscent of my grandfather's.

I think that this tallit will always be my link to a trip unlike any other, a visit to the president's home that I will never forget.

**Yitz Rubin** returned to Israel in 1971 as a volunteer English teacher for a program called *Sherut La'am* (Service to the People, akin to the Peace Corps), and met his wife Carol then. They have been married thirty-two years and have three children, David, Jonathan, and Talia. The National Sales Manager for a large apparel company, Mr. Rubin has lived in Syosset, New York, since 1978. The Rubins belong to Midway Jewish Center in Syosset, where they volunteer, socialize, and daven. It is there that Mr. Rubin confronts his emotional ties to his tallit.

# From Israel with Love

*Laurie Kimmelstiel*

During my very first trip to Israel some thirty-three years ago, I decided to purchase a tallit for my dear father. I had traveled to Israel as part of a group of campers from the Leadership Training Camp (LTC) of the Cejwin Camps of Port Jervis, New York.

This seven-week immersion in Israeli life and culture was the culmination of a multisummer program I was privileged to be a part of, to learn leadership skills that could be applied back at camp and within the Jewish community. The summer in Israel was our third summer together for this cadre of thirty-five teenagers. We were a close-knit group of friends who often got together during the school year for socializing and parties. To this day, I count many members of this group among my dearest and closest friends.

I wanted to buy the tallit in Mea Shearim, Jerusalem's most religious quarter, where Yiddish—not Hebrew—was the lingua franca of the neighborhood. So I asked the assistance of one of the boys in the group who spoke German. A son of Holocaust survivors, he spoke German as his first language and he seemed the most competent to deal with the Yiddish-speaking shopkeeper. I hoped he could both guide my choice from a male perspective and help me guarantee a decent price and a quality tallit. He willingly obliged and was kind enough to help me choose a lovely large woolen black and white tallit for my Dad.

My father lovingly wore his Israeli tallit over the

years. I always admired its simple stripes, smooth wool weave, and traditional appearance. It was a very special gift for my father from his only daughter's first visit to Jerusalem.

Several years passed. I attended college and graduate school and lost touch with some of my friends from that first trip to Israel. But these were not friends who easily slipped from memory. Periodically, we would call and meet again at weddings and simchas. And some friendships are just meant to last.

And so it was—on Yom Yerushalayim in 1981, ten years after I had bought this tallit in Jerusalem—that I stood under my father's tallit, to marry my *beshert*, that wonderful German-speaking young man who helped me choose and purchase it in Jerusalem.

**Laurie Kimmelstiel** is a fiber artist who lives in White Plains, New York, with her husband Fred and three children. She makes hand-woven Judaic textiles and specializes in the design and creation of one-of-a-kind tallitot. She also is a knitter and writer and the coauthor of *Exquisite Little Knits* (Lark Books, 2004). She is a member of Young Israel of White Plains.

# A Tallit from the Holy Land That Sanctifies a Family

*Rabbi Andy Koren*

As an engagement present, my aunt gave me some money and asked that I spend it on something meaningful, perhaps a tallit. She knew that Michal (my fiancée) and I would be traveling to Israel in the winter of 1990–1991 so that I could meet the Israeli side of what was about to become "our" family. Traveling to Israel at that time was hardly encouraged. Iraq had invaded Kuwait in August of 1990, and the United States was about to launch a ground offensive to liberate Kuwait. Anticipating the worst, gas masks had been distributed to all Israelis. Our Israeli engagement party had a surreal feeling, as conversations shifted between the upcoming simcha and what to do in the event of a chemical attack.

Our trip to Israel ended before the ground offensive began. While we were there, we bought a rainbow-colored tallit from the Gabrieli tallit shop. It was an enormous tallit, and prior to using it for prayers, we decided that we would first use it as our chuppah. At the same time, we wondered what it would be like if this tallit became an important component of each of our family's Jewish celebrations.

Those thoughts have translated into a very beautiful reality over the past fourteen years. We were married under our tallit in the summer of 1991. In the summer of 1993, I wore the tallit when I was ordained as a rabbi. My sister and her husband were married under the tallit, as were my brother and his wife, and three of our cousins. When my mom became bat mitzvah as an adult, not only was the tallit there, but she had also purchased her own similarly colored Gabrieli tallit to wear during services. On the day of his brit milah, our son was wrapped in the tallit as we joyously brought him into the room. The tallit then became the covering for Elijah's chair.

My sister's sons were likewise wrapped in the tallit on the days that they entered into the covenant first established between God and Abraham. Our daughter received her name in temple with the tallit covering her. The same was true for my brother's baby daughter. We had a beautiful baby naming for her and, like her older cousins, she was blessed and entered the covenant connected to our family tallit.

Our tallit has become another common thread running through the story of our family. It binds one generation of the family to another, and has become a Jewish connecting point for a generation of cousins.

**Rabbi Andy Koren** recently joined the staff of Temple Emanuel in Greensboro, North Carolina, where he lives with his wife Michal and their children, Avishai and Shiri. For his first ten years as a rabbi, he primarily worked with college students, serving as the Director of North Carolina Hillel (1993–1995) and as the rabbi for the Hillel Foundation at the University of Florida (1998–2003). From 1995 to 1998, he served as program associate for the Wexner Foundation in Columbus, Ohio, concentrating on Jewish leadership development as well as recruitment for the Wexner Graduate Fellowship Program.

# A Day of Mixed Feelings

*Riette Thomas Smith*

My husband and I were enjoying our first trip to Israel. First we had spent time in Jerusalem, and then we rented a car to tour the country.

One day, when we were in Tel Aviv, we were returning from the Museums of the Diaspora to the shopping district and our hotel. We enjoyed wandering through the busy streets filled with shops, the bustling activity all around, the sidewalks crowded with babies in strollers in front of open-air restaurants and coffeehouses. We were in search of Gabrieli's, so that I could look at tallitot, hoping to purchase my very first. Although I was sixty, I was buying my first tallit ever: I was a woman and a classical Reform Jewess, and when I was coming of age you never saw a woman wearing a tallit or a yarmulke. I was especially excited about making this momentous purchase in Israel.

My husband and I had just arrived at the shop, when suddenly the street was filled with activity of another kind altogether: Sirens were blaring, armed soldiers were everywhere, many different types of military vehicles were rolling down the street in a determined, swift-moving line, and ambulances were interspersed with the military entourage. The woman helping us turned on the radio and translated the news for us: A suicide bomber had blown himself up in a popular coffeehouse just two blocks away. Two young professional women, who were also mothers, were dead. Their toddlers had been playing outside in the sun while this bombing occurred. In addition to these two deaths, plus that of the bomber, forty-two others had been wounded.

We asked the woman about her fears living here in Israel, but her replies surprised us. She spoke of being more fearful in New York City: "You have just as many guns, but they are hidden. You have just as much random violence, but it is not by a hidden enemy acting for a cause."

In addition, this single parent had two sons in the army. We asked if she were not fearful for her sons. She said, "At least here we know what we die for."

After we had completed our purchases, we kept talking about the situation. Then the woman gave us directions to get around the site of the tragedy and back to our hotel a block on the other side.

Each time I wear my tallit, this experience is clear in my mind. Like a flashback, I feel the fear once again, and hear in my mind the calming, courageous words of this Israeli woman. This happened several years ago, when violence was not an everyday occurrence in Israel, as it is today. The faith the Israeli woman and mother expressed to me that day envelopes me whenever I don my tallit for services. The tallit is aquamarine and black, hand-woven, with a yarmulke to match. These colors are reminiscent both of the sea at Tel Aviv and the grief and mourning I feel for those injured and killed that day I purchased my first tallit. This mirrors my feelings of joy at being in Israel buying the tallit and my sadness at the violence.

**Riette Thomas Smith**, who lives in Bloomington, Indiana, is a marriage, family, and sex therapist. She and her husband belong to Congregation Beth Shalom. They have two children and two grandchildren.

# The Gift

## *Allan Rabinowitz*

On Simchat Torah, at the small egalitarian synagogue I attend in Jerusalem, I sat near the table on which the Torah lay open. As is our tradition, the children were called forward for a collective blessing, beneath a tallit spread over them as a canopy. I removed mine, which is huge. As we held it above those children, I turned to my wife and saw that she had tears in her eyes, as I suddenly did.

An old woman named Hava had given me that tallit more than twenty years earlier when, as a yeshiva student in Jerusalem, I lived in a blocklike stucco apartment complex. My kitchen window looked across the rubble-filled central courtyard into hers. Often I saw her enter her kitchen and take her bright, flowered apron off its hook. With round cheeks, wire-rimmed glasses, and a bun of silver hair, she looked like a picture on a cookie package. My roommate Glenn and I nicknamed her Mrs. Fields.

In my first exchange with her, on the stairs, she said, "When you hang your laundry on the line, it drips on the laundry of the woman below. Check first before you hang it." We were just one more set of students who wandered through this apartment building.

Colorful prints hung on her kitchen's eggshell-colored wall. Every Friday evening, on a little cabinet against the wall, she lit Shabbat candles. Occasionally, as Hava glided through the creamy kitchen light, I envied that bubble of comfort and order, which sharply contrasted with our eternally dish-filled sink.

Among the courtyard debris beneath Hava's window, cats gathered every day at dusk, and jockeyed for position with yowling, hissing, and claw strikes. They grew taut when she slid her kitchen window open, and sprang forward and up when she tossed out a daily ration of food scraps.

Glenn and I studied at the yeshiva all day. Glenn diligently awoke early every morning for *Shacharit* prayers at school before classes began. But I resisted prayer, and wrote in the early hours. One cold, dark winter morning, just after Glenn had left, there was a hard pounding on my door. As I opened it, Hava frantically beckoned me to follow her.

When we entered her neat apartment, she tugged me by my sleeve to the bathroom and gestured for me to open the door. But something was blocking it. Wiggling it back and forth, I was able at last to thrust my head past the doorjamb. To my surprise, an old, heavy man with bulging eyes, clutching his heart and gasping, was slumped against the door in pajamas. He must have been bed-ridden all this time. I told Hava to call for an ambulance, and futilely practiced the little CPR technique I remembered from a first-aid course. In the living room a neighbor named Rachel comforted Hava as she wept.

The ambulance driver asked me to help carry the man down the stairs in a wheelchair. I grabbed its front end. The sick man wore an oxygen mask. As I backed gingerly down the stairs, he labored for breath. His belly bulged out of a partially unbuttoned pajama shirt. His hair was wispy and gray, highlighting jagged black eyebrows. Above the mask, large blue eyes fixed upon my eyes. Those eyes closed before we reached the ambulance.

Later that day, Rachel knocked on my door and told me that the man never reopened his eyes, and died on the way to the hospital. From the front seat, Hava had heard the paramedic's efforts to revive him. I, a stranger, was the last person this man saw.

The many neighbors who made shiva calls to Hava were mostly old and hunched over. When I visited in the evening, there was hardly space to sit. The room was stuffy and warm, despite the harsh winds outside. One wall was lined with shelves filled with volumes of the Talmud, the Torah with commentaries, and additional religious texts. A breakfront on another wall was filled with painted plates, cups, and delicate porcelain animals.

Hava sat on a cushion on the floor. She looked at me and nodded, then leaned over and whispered something to a young man who sat beside her. He looked to be a few years older than me, with wild dark curls that obscured his small kippah. He wore brown slippers, and his plaid shirt had been ripped near the collar, as is the Jewish custom for mourners.

He rose and approached me. "I'm Avi, the son," he said in English with a gurgling Israeli accent. I offered condolences, in Hebrew. He nodded. "Where you from in the States?" he asked, again in English.

"New Jersey."

"Really? I'm in New York."

"How long are you there for?"

He shrugged. "I'm just there. I'm a painter." From his back pocket he pulled out a business card, with his name and studio address written in blue brush-stroked letters. "When you come back, come visit my studio. I have some shows coming up."

"Thanks. I'm not sure when I'll be back."

"Neither am I."

A heavy-set woman cut between us and engulfed him in her arms as she sniffled out her sorrow.

Someone asked me to come to an early minyan the next morning for *Shacharit* prayers, and without thinking I said I would. When I showed up the next morning, Hava, in slippers and a ripped housedress, was sitting on her cushion sipping tea.

Men wrapped tefillin on their arms, each man draped in a tallit. Avi stood there wearing neither, only a kippah, like me. At that point, I did not wear tefillin, and did not own a tallit. If Avi had not been there, I would have felt like an imposter. Even so, I expected to be accosted or scolded.

Hava brought over a tallit, in a beautiful blue velvet bag, and I used that. I was surprised that she brought it to me, rather than to her son. After the prayers, a man quietly offered me his tefillin. I accepted, let him wrap them on my arm, said the blessings, then removed them.

I showed up every morning for prayers. Hava handed me the tallit, and the same man offered his tefillin after he had finished praying. They felt unwieldy on me, yet in the tallit I felt embraced in a membrane that enhanced the power of the words.

Avi left immediately after the seven-day shiva period. I again saw Hava puttering around her kitchen. One morning she again knocked on my door. "I have something for you," she said. "Please come." In her apartment, again neatly arranged, we sat at a small nicked table in the kitchen. She offered me tea, and served it with cookies. Then she excused herself, left the room, and returned a moment later carrying a white plastic bag.

"Moshe was a real Torah scholar," she said as she sat again. "He would study fourteen, fifteen hours a day. Students took turns studying with him. Like dancing partners." I felt awkward as she rambled. "Sometimes I put a cup of tea by him and he never noticed until I said, 'Moshele, your tea's getting cold.' Then he would look up, with his eyes so wide like they just wanted to drink in every word in the book, and cock his head. Like a puppy." I pictured those blue eyes facing me, drinking in only fear.

"In the thirties students gathered around him in basements, secretly; Stalin already hunted religious Jews. Finally he and our first son—Ya'acov—landed in work camps in Siberia. I didn't even know Moshe was still alive until 1949. I was walking along Jaffa Road, and a man in front of me was walking so slowly, with a book open before him. Then he cocked his head, and I cried out, 'Dear God, it's Moshe.' He turned, and we both screamed there on the sidewalk. That's when I learned that Ya'acov had died in a labor camp, and I cried over him as if I had never thought that before."

That was an amazing story, I mumbled, "and beautiful."

"Not so beautiful, believe me," she said. "I hated this place. Some of Moshe's old students wanted to bring him to New York to teach. But he said he was staying here, no matter what. 'No matter what?' I asked him. 'So that another son should die? It's better if he dies in uniform?'" She smiled. "My son's in New York now. He's a painter."

"Yes, he told me."

"He wants me to go there," she said.

"And are you going?"

She shrugged and put down her tea. "Oh, Moshe was so hurt that Avi dropped kashrut and Shabbat, after what he'd gone through just to be here. He kept reminding him of how Ya'acov always studied. I said to Moshe, 'You think we can influence these young ones? Forget it. That's the way things are.'"

She reached into the white plastic bag and pulled out the embroidered blue velvet bag containing the tallit I had been praying in all week. "I thought I'd give this to Avi. But he'd probably use it to clean his brushes. You're the only one beside my husband who's ever worn it."

In shock, I took and stroked the bag, barely able to thank her. Enveloped in this broad tallit, which belonged to a man I never knew, yet whose eyes I saw staring into death, I had prayed to open myself to God. And now this tallit was pressed upon me.

Before the next Shabbat, I bought flowers for Hava. She protested, then profusely thanked me. Later I saw the flowers, from across the courtyard, standing in a vase on her kitchen counter, opposite my window. It struck me as a strange place to display flowers.

I still had Avi's business card. I wrote to him that I had his father's tallit; it was his for the asking.

"Thanks, I'll keep that in mind," he answered. "If you visit New Jersey, come see my studio." He never did request the tallit, and I never saw his studio.

I saw Hava passing by on the stairs, puttering in her kitchen, feeding the cats. When I offered to pick up odd items for her at the nearby grocery, or to move heavy objects in her apartment, she refused my offer with thanks and smiles. And she never invited me again for tea, during the following months when I plunged into Jewish sources and learned to pray.

Sometimes, wrapped in my tallit, I imagined Moshe rocking in it, saying the same prayers, his blue eyes bright and fervent. This tallit spread over my bride and me as a chuppah, and surrounded my son after his brit milah. He was among the gaggle of kids who approached the Torah under it. Next Simchat Torah, I will make certain that I again sit in the front.

**Allan Rabinowitz**, formerly a journalist, became a licensed tour guide and travel writer after making aliyah (with stints as a kibbutz worker, a construction worker, a yeshiva student, a writing teacher, and a soldier), and has lectured widely on Israel in synagogues, schools, and universities. For six years he wrote a regular travel column for the *Jerusalem Post*, and recently completed his first novel, based on the life of Jeremiah the prophet. He lives in Jerusalem with his family.

# Blue and White and Respected

*Batsheva Pomerantz*

One of the best-known examples of the tallit stands proudly in the yards of Jewish schools and atop Jewish institutions throughout the world. This tallit is the flag of the State of Israel, which also represents the Jewish people wherever they may be.

A symbol of the Jewish people's yearning for Zion, the design—light-blue stripes on the margins of a field of white with a Star of David (*Magen David*) in the center—was already well recognized when it became the official flag of the Jewish state in October 1948.

Already in 1885, the blue-and-white flag was used to mark the third anniversary of Rishon Le-Zion, a town in the land of Israel established by early pioneers. Blue-and-white flags with the word *Maccabee* in the center of the Magen David had actually been unfurled at the dedication of the Bnai Zion hall in Boston in 1891.

The flag became prominent when used by the Zionist movement during the First Zionist Congress held in Basel, Switzerland, in 1897. David Wolfson, one of the organizers, is credited with creating the Zionist flag, while he pondered how to decorate the hall. He was looking for colors that would be discernable to Jews everywhere, a people careful to avoid idols and images.

Before Wolfson's design was unfurled, Theodore Herzl, visionary and founder of the Zionist movement, had suggested a white background symbolizing purity and a new life, with seven golden stars to represent the seven-hour workday. His idea was not well received.

Legend has it that Wolfson stood up and proclaimed: "What do we have to search for—here is our national flag." As he spoke, he waved his own tallit, thus presenting the national flag—a field of white with stripes on its margins. He then ordered his staff to produce a blue-and-white flag with a Magen David in the center.

Whether the men were actually adorned in their tallit shawls during preparations for the Zionist Congress is a matter of conjecture. But Wolfson was certainly aware of the symbolism of the Magen David and the light-blue stripes. The Magen David became recognized as a Jewish symbol toward the end of the Middle Ages, when authorities allowed the Jews of Prague to use it on their synagogue and as the community's seal. In the mid–seventeenth century, the Vienna Jewish community adopted the six-pointed star. Austrian-Jewish poet Ludwig August Frankl published the poem "Judah's Colors" in 1864 about the blue-and-white colors representing the people of Israel. This was more than thirty years before the First Zionist Congress.

The stripes' light-blue color, known in Hebrew as *techelet*, is reminiscent of the *techelet* thread in the tzitzit. The tzitzit are fringes required by the Torah to be attached to four-cornered garments, and are on the tallit, too. In ancient times production of the *techelet* dye was a booming business along the Mediterranean coast. It was prepared during Roman times for Roman royalty, and its production by Jews went underground. With the Arab conquest of the Land of Israel in the seventh century, the infrastructure of the *techelet* industry was destroyed and its production ceased. (Research in recent generations based on textual, historical, nautical study and chemical analysis has shown evidence that the *techelet* dye was extracted from a specific snail—the murex trunculus.)

In the Talmud, Rabbi Meir says that the *techelet* signifies the grandeur of the world. It reminds us of the depths of the color of light, and the Heavenly Throne of Glory, and thus of God's presence in the world. Rabbi Yehuda, son of Rabbi Ilai, said: "Whenever the people of Israel look at this *techelet*, they are reminded of the commandments on the two tablets of law," since the *techelet* is the color of the tablets and looking at the *techelet* thread prompts us to observe mitzvot. *Techelet* and white were the colors of the garments of the high priest, reminding Jews of purity, and thus symbolizing the spirituality of the Jewish people.

The Zionist mission to create a Jewish state needed a symbol of purity and spirituality—both ever-present in the tallit. The Magen David was added as a Jewish symbol recognized by both Jews and non-Jews.

After the establishment of the State of Israel in May 1948, a competition was held to create a flag that differed from the Zionist flag to avoid confusion. The committee received 164 suggestions, most of them based on the white field and blue stripes. Some came up with the idea of having a compact Zionist flag in the corner with other elements in the background, similar to the flags of the British Commonwealth nations depicting a miniature British flag with added details. After months of debate by both Israeli and Diaspora leaders, it was finally decided to adopt the Zionist flag as the flag of the State of Israel.

Nowhere is the connection between the tallit and the Israeli flag felt more intensely than when both are draped over the coffin of a soldier who fell in defense of the State of Israel. The flag of Israel, intertwined with the tallit, symbolizes the sovereignty of Israel for which the Jewish people have dreamt and prayed for nearly two thousand years.

**Batsheva Pomerantz** is a freelance writer, journalist, and editor. Her feature articles on Jewish identity, Zionist history, Holocaust commemoration, and Jewish communities have appeared in publications in the Diaspora, the *Jerusalem Post*, and the Israeli Hebrew press. She came to Israel as a child from New York and lives with her husband and children in Jerusalem.

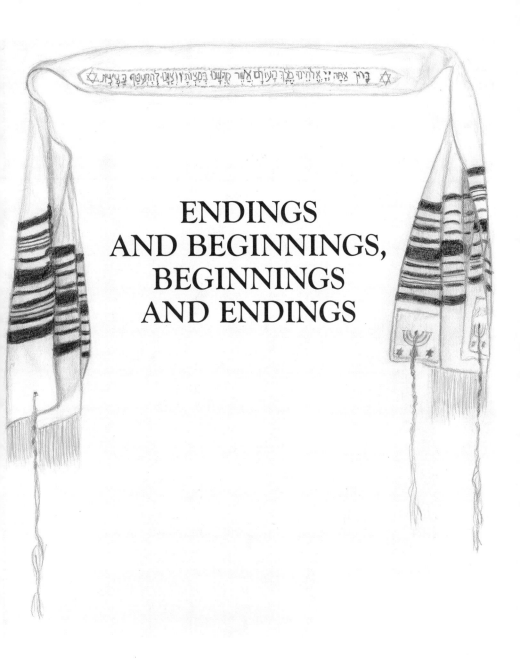

# ENDINGS
# AND BEGINNINGS,
# BEGINNINGS
# AND ENDINGS

# Against All Odds

## Debra W. Smith

DottieandAdele, AdeleandDottie. I am used to uttering their names in one breath, as if they were one person. While they are as distinct as night and day, they are as connected as branches on the same tree. They do not share the bonds of blood, but they each have a profound love of Torah and Jewish learning—a passion that infuses their relationship with holiness. The *etz hayim*, the tree of life, has deep and strong roots in the relationship of each of these women to Judaism and to each other.

Shortly after moving into the newly opened Lester Senior Community at MetroWest, in Whippany, New Jersey, Dottie and Adele befriended each other. When they first met, Adele confided in Dottie that she was fulfilling a long-time desire to learn Hebrew by taking a series of beginner lessons. It was only natural for Dottie to invite Adele to join her at weekly services in the Lester chapel. This was an invitation Adele accepted eagerly. She has been there every week, with rare exceptions, ever since.

The women, who live down the hall from each other, became good friends and have been sitting together at services and in the dining room for the past four years. Early on in their relationship, they discovered that they had a lifelong dream in common: to become a bat mitzvah. They decided to pursue this dream, and the culminating ceremony, together. And they each wanted to take on the obligation of wearing a tallit as part of that milestone life-cycle event.

A colleague of mine brought the three of us together for a trial Hebrew lesson, and thus began a profoundly meaningful spiritual journey for all of us. I learned at our first meeting that these two women were determined to become b'not mitzvah. I readily agreed to serve as their tutor, to help them prepare for their "coming of age" ceremony, and to officiate at the wonderful simcha.

Dottie and Adele have given new and true meaning to the concept of *hevruta* (partner) study: They were study partners throughout the whole year leading up to their B'not Mitzvah. Dottie, whose grasp of Hebrew was very strong, helped Adele learn to read Hebrew with increasing fluency. Adele, who loves to sing, picked up the trope early in the process with the assistance of a tape made by my husband, Neil. She became our "Queen of the Chant." Dottie, meanwhile, preferred to read her portion of the Haftarah.

Each one's skills complemented the other's, and up until six weeks before the Big Event, neither of the women missed a single lesson. Wednesdays at 2 p.m. was our special time. We always studied at a table in the small chapel, within view of the *ner tamid* (the eternal light), whose steady flame was an equal match to the passion for learning burning in the women's hearts.

One Wednesday about six weeks before the B'not Mitzvah, I arrived for our weekly study session to find Adele waiting for me alone, looking utterly forlorn. She greeted me with the following words: "I am not sure how to tell you this, but Dottie fell and broke her hip yesterday. She is in the hospital now undergoing surgery and will be going to a rehab from there." We looked at each other with the same thought: What about the B'not Mitzvah? Would Dottie recover in time to fulfill her life-long dream? The date the women had chosen for the B'not Mitzvah, December 7, the second Shabbat of Hanukkah 2002, was halfway between each of their upcoming birthdays. Adele would have just celebrated her eighty-third birthday and Dottie would be approaching her eighty-fifth.

By the next morning when I spoke with Dottie's daughter, Cynthia, the upshot of this unfortunate event was clear: Dottie would indeed be celebrating her Bat Mitzvah. The dream would most certainly become a reality. Throughout her recovery from surgery and her time in rehab, Dottie studied her Haftarah and her parts in the Shabbat service. Her son-in-law, Dr. Howard Schwartz, brought her Hebrew books to the hospital and studied with her on a daily basis. Dottie laughed at the recollection that when her doctor came to see her on rounds, he found her studying her Haftarah. The two of them then compared Hebrew reading skills by reading for each other! On a more somber note, though, Dottie admitted that she was plagued by constant worry that her lifelong ambition—to become a bat mitzvah—would be a casualty of this unforeseeable accident.

The time leading up to the Big Day also had its worries for Adele, who developed total laryngitis ten days pre–B'not Mitzvah. Refusing to allow myself to succumb to worry, I focused on preparing the service, the Dvar Torah, and my Torah readings. I had my hands full with all this, so I stepped back and left the physical recovery of my students to G-d, trusting that everything would turn out fine.

Dottie came home from rehab about two weeks before the B'not Mitzvah. She rapidly progressed from walker to cane. She walked completely unassisted to the bimah (my guess: she was floating on air!) to bless and don her tallit, receive her aliyah, and later read her Haftarah on the day of the B'not Mitzvah. Adele fully recovered her voice and chanted loudly, clearly, and very proudly. The day was memorable for everyone present. A lifelong dream, shared by the two friends, had been fulfilled in grand style.

The women's tallitot were quite distinctive, each nothing like the other. Each tallit had brought a life full circle for its owner. Adele shopped with her sons, Mickey and Sandy, to purchase her tallit at a local Judaica shop. Her tallit, with its matching bag, depicts the city of Jerusalem in an array of purples and pinks. She recalls that she had bought her sons and then her grandsons their tallitot when each became a bar mitzvah. Now it was her sons' turn to do the same for her. How proud they are of what she has accomplished in such a short time!

"G-d gave me years," reflects Adele gratefully, "and I have been fortunate enough to accomplish a lifelong ambition that I always longed for and never could complete."

Dottie's tallit was one she had given to her granddaughter, Melissa, on the occasion of her Bat Mitzvah, a milestone it was uncertain that Melissa would ever reach. Melissa, who underwent a lifesaving liver transplant at age ten, did indeed become a bat mitzvah and recently marked the twentieth anniversary of that new lease on life. She and her husband, Brett, have become parents themselves now: Melissa gave birth to their first child, a son named Jesse, about a year ago. Melissa proudly presented her grandmother with the same beautiful tallit, designed in varying shades of pink, that Dottie had given her years ago.

"Having Melissa here with me on this special day to present me with 'our' tallit meant everything to me," Dottie says, beaming.

"It was meant for us to meet and do this together. I just know that," adds Dottie. Adele smiles and nods in agreement. DottieandAdele have not stopped there. They continue their studies with me, now joined by thirty of their neighbors. We meet weekly in the chapel, within sight of and fueled by the light of that same ner tamid.

**Adele Kaplan** and **Dorothy Schram** are residents of the Lester Senior Housing Community in Whippany, New Jersey.

**Adele**, a former resident of Edison, New Jersey, worked for Vector Engineering as private secretary to the President and later as Assistant to the Comptroller. She has two sons, Mickey and Sandy, and seven grandchildren.

**Dottie**, a Little Falls resident for many years, was part of a tap dance group called the Top Hatters that performed throughout northern New Jersey. She and her late husband Joseph owned and operated a luncheonette in Paterson, New Jersey. She later worked for the Bell Telephone Company. She has two children, Cynthia and Sheldon, six grandchildren, and one great-grandchild.

# Epilogue:
# Tallit of My Heart

I have a dear, long-time friend, Elaine Schechter Luscombe. We should all be fortunate enough to have an Elaine in our lives. Elaine was the first friend I made when I moved to Long Valley, and I probably would have run home to Westchester, New York, if she hadn't been there as I struggled to adjust to life in the "wilds of New Jersey." Our family has shared Thanksgiving and Passover with Elaine and her husband Eric for the past twenty-four years. They are our New Jersey family. Spending holidays with them has given a sense of stability and continuity to our lives. We have created traditions together and those traditions ground our lives. Elaine gives new and true meaning to the expression *eshet chayil* (woman of valor).

Throughout those years, Elaine has been an avid quilter. Quilting is her passion, a labor of love, and her quilts are magnificent. Elaine quilted my younger daughter, Dana's, baby quilt and has made quilts for both Elana and Dana on special occasions in their lives, such as graduations and their B'not Mitzvah.

Though I have spoken with many talented and creative tallit-makers while writing this book, I never felt comfortable asking any one of them to make a tallit for me. They didn't know me; they hadn't traveled with me on my life's journey. Elaine has been there at every bend and turn over the past two-plus decades. Elaine was the only one who could make this one-of-a-kind tallit, a tallit that sprang from the same impulse that guided me to compile the essays and poems in *Every Tallit Tells a Tale*. I approached her with hesitation, hating to take advantage; but true friend that she is, she responded with eagerness and delight.

We have begun to plan the design and colors of the tallit together. I know it will be beautiful and I know it will reflect the relationship I have grown to have with G-d and with the Jewish community. It will be the "tallit of my heart," and its tzitzit will guide me on the next leg of my journey.

I have decided to honor this tallit in a special ceremony before wearing it for the first time. I will bless it and place it on my shoulders in the presence of the community I have fashioned for myself over the years of my Jewish journey.

As part of that special ceremony, I will acknowledge my chosen community: friends, study partners, professional colleagues, rabbis, mentors, students, teachers, and, of course, my family. They have evolved into a very intimate community, and I have shared the secrets and yearnings of my heart with so many of them. They are a community that has supported my journey and encouraged me to go forward when that has seemed too hard to do. They have enfolded me and helped me travel from being a seeker on the fringe of Judaism, to one who has accepted and made her own so many aspects of Jewish practice, including the acceptance of the fringes of the tallit and what they represent. My community has sheltered me and enfolded my family and me in its life in much the same way that my new tallit will embrace me and enfold me in G-d's arms. It is only fitting that the "tallit of my heart" should be my partner in prayer among the "community of my heart."

Amen. Selah.

—Debra W. Smith

# About the Editor

Debra W. Smith, an inspiring Jewish life educator, is the winner of the prestigious Leo Brody Award, presented to an outstanding professional in the field of Jewish education. A resident of Long Valley, NJ, Debra is Director of the Hirschhorn Senior Adult Jewish Education Program at the United Jewish Communities of MetroWest in Whippany, New Jersey. She is a certified lay religious leader through the IMUN Lay Leaders Institute of the United Synagogue of Conservative Judaism. Debra is also a faculty member in Judaic Studies at DOROT: The University Without Walls, in New York City. Debra's passion for Jewish life mirrors that of her biblical namesake.

Debra and her husband, Dr. Neil Smith, have two grown daughters, Elana and Dana.

Debra loves hearing from readers. She can be reached at hineni77@aol.com.

# To Order Additional Copies
## of
## *Every Tallit Tells a Tale*

*Copy this form, fill it out,
and send it with your check or money order to:*

**Stella Hart, Inc.
105 Shady Lane
Randolph NJ 07869
Tel: 973–895–3356 • stellahart@blast.net**

**Please send [    ] copies of *Every Tallit Tells a Tale*
to me at the following address:**

Name:_____

Address: _____

City:_____ State: _____ Zip: _____

Telephone: _____

e-mail address:_____

**Price:** $18.00 USD apiece, plus $3.50 shipping for first book.
Add $1.00 extra for shipping for each additional book
(shipping for 2 books, $4.50; shipping for 3 books, $5.50; etc.).

**Sales tax:** Please add 6% for books shipped to New Jersey addresses.